P9-DVQ-106

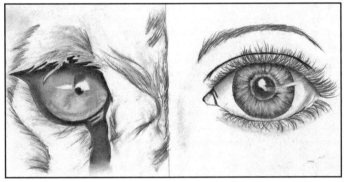

Cover Art: "Eyes" by Ivan Villagomez

NEW VOICES

A COLLECTION OF STUDENT ESSAYS

25th Edition

STRETCH COMPOSITION PROGRAM
DEPARTMENT OF ENGLISH
CALIFORNIA STATE UNIVERSITY, NORTHRIDGE

SANDRA JACKSON, *Editor*
AMY REYNOLDS, *Co-Editor*
AMBER NORWOOD, *Associate Editor*

Visit New Voices/Wings Online:
http://newvoices-wings.haydenmcneil.com

HAYDEN
HM
McNEIL

Hayden-McNeil Sustainability

Hayden-McNeil's standard paper stock uses a minimum of 30% post-consumer waste. We offer higher % options by request, including a 100% recycled stock. Additionally, Hayden-McNeil Custom Digital provides authors with the opportunity to convert print products to a digital format. Hayden-McNeil is part of a larger sustainability initiative through Macmillan Higher Ed. Visit http://sustainability.macmillan.com to learn more.

Copyright © 2016 by California State University, Northridge

All rights reserved.

Permission in writing must be obtained from the publisher before any part of this work may be reproduced or transmitted in any form or by any means, electronic or mechanical, including photocopying and recording, or by any information storage or retrieval system.

Printed in the United States of America

10 9 8 7 6 5 4 3 2 1

ISBN 978-0-7380-7886-1

Hayden-McNeil Publishing
14903 Pilot Drive
Plymouth, MI 48170
www.hmpublishing.com

Jackson 7886-1 F15

ACKNOWLEDGEMENTS

Many thanks to all who make *New Voices* possible:

CSUN Administration
Dr. Elizabeth Say, Dean of Humanities
Dr. Elizabeth T. Adams, Associate Vice-President, Undergraduate Studies

The English Department
Dr. Jackie Stallcup, English Department Chair
Dr. Irene Clark, Director of Composition
Department Administration: Marlene Cooksey, Frank De La Santo, Antoinette Mangum, Wendy Say, Marjie Seagoe

Hayden-McNeil Publishing
Barb DeVore, Senior Managing Editor

The Matador Bookstore
Amy Berger, Manager

New Voices Editorial Board

James Bezerra	John Kubler	Amy Reynolds
Pamela Bourgeois	Stephanie Lim	Jennifer Rodrick
Mona Houghton	Donna Marsh	Terri Silverberg
Sandra Jackson	Amber Norwood	Elyce Wakerman

Associate Editor
Amber Norwood

Assistant Editors
James Bezerra
Stephanie Lim

Photographs & Other Artwork
Kathy Leslie, Donna Marsh, Amy Reynolds, Marjie Seagoe, Ani Muradyan
Cover Art: Ivan Villagomez

Judges
Karen Abramowitz, Mary Marca, Debra Mercado

ACKNOWLEDGEMENTS

Special thanks to Elyce Wakerman for hosting the *New Voices* Reading.

Many thanks to our families for their patience, especially Ces & Moss.

Most of all, thanks to the many students, published and unpublished, who share their new voices with us each year.

JESSE ALEXANDER ALFARO

2014 RECIPIENT OF

THE PAMELA BOURGEOIS PRIZE

FOR WRITING EXCELLENCE IN THE FIRST YEAR

With his English Instructor, Kelli Rowley, and Dr. Pamela Bourgeois, founder and managing editor of *New Voices* (retired).

The $250 prize is awarded to the best essay written by a Stretch Composition student, published in either *New Voices* or *Wings*.

Alfaro's winning essay,
"Walter White/Heisenberg: The 21st Century Version
of Dr. Jekyll And Mr. Hyde"
appeared in the 2014 edition of *Wings*.

NEW VOICES WRITING AWARDS

The following students will receive prizes sponsored by the Matador Bookstore at the Publication Ceremony in Fall 2015:

SECTION 1: CONSIDERING LITERACY
First Place: Jing Huang, "My English Journey"

SECTION 2: VALUING EDUCATION
First Place: Angela Pham, "A Day in the Life of a CSUN Student"

SECTION 3: ANALYZING GENDER
First Place: Liz Herwig, "Gay Marriage and the Constitution"

SECTION 4: EXAMINING SOCIAL MEDIA
Honorable Mention: Alexandra-Joyce Porte, "The Human Experience"

SECTION 5: CONTEMPLATING FOOD
First Place: Abeer Almutairi, "Drinking Coffee Alone in America"

SECTION 6: CONFRONTING ILLNESS
First Place: Elizabeth Altounian, "Ebola and Social Media"

SECTION 7: TELLING DOG TALES
First Place: Joshua Corona, "Dog Days"

SECTION 8: REFLECTING ON WRITING
Honorable Mention: Yareli Barahona, "How English Composition Has Helped Me"

SECTION 9 (ONLINE): RESPONDING TO TEXTS
Honorable Mention: Ali Alawadhi, "More Than a Friend"

COVER ART AWARD
Ivan Villagomez, "Eyes"

JUDGES
Karen Abramowitz, SAT Lab/SI Coordinator, Learning Resource Center, CSUN

Mary Marca, Faculty, English Department, CSUN (Retired)

Debra Mercado, UDWPE Assistant Coordinator; Faculty, Academic First Year Experiences, CSUN

TABLE OF CONTENTS

NEW VOICES ONLINE
<http://newvoices-wings.haydenmcneil.com>

MATADOR BOOKSTORE

is a proud sponsor of the 2015 edition of New Voices

Stop by the Matador Bookstore for 30% off bestsellers every day!

"A great book should leave you with many experiences, and slightly exhausted at the end. You live several lives while reading."

William Styron

Matador Bookstore

Bookstore Complex | 818.677.2932 | matadorbookstore.com

f /matadorbookstore

RHETORICAL TABLE OF CONTENTS

SECTION 1:
CONSIDERING LITERACY

QUICK WRITE:

What does it mean to be "literate"? Who or what has affected your path to literacy, either positively or negatively?

NOTES, RESPONSES, & IDEAS

> *In my opinion, literacy is the ability to make some connections between our own experiences and the things we read.*

JING HUANG

Instructor: Anna Dawahare

MY ENGLISH JOURNEY

I applied to participate in the 2+2 program at my university in China two years ago. The 2+2 program meant that after I had studied in China for two years, I needed to study in the United States for two more years. Most of my friends wondered why I decided to study abroad because they thought that it would be very difficult for me to adapt. More importantly, they knew that English was not my first language and thought I would have lots of problems in reading and writing. One of my friends even asked me, "If you cannot understand the assignments, how will you do them?" Actually, I did not know how to reply to my friend. I knew the difficulties in studying abroad: I could not understand English texts, so I would not do well in the assignments in English and so on. Most of the difficulties would be with reading and writing. Nevertheless, I still decided to participate in the 2+2 program. I firmly believed that this program could enrich my life experience and broaden my horizons. On the journey of my life, I want to challenge myself and learn more about the world.

Even though Chinese is my mother language, I began to learn English when I was a five-year-old child and my mother sent me to class to learn English. What an interesting class it was! The teacher, a lovely woman, taught English by playing some interesting games, singing songs, and so on. I still remember that the first word I learned was "apple." At first, the teacher showed us the picture of an apple, then told some funny stories about apples. At last, the teacher taught a song about the apple to help us deeply remember the word "apple." This was an interesting way to teach children to remember the words.

When I was a high-school student, I received a *Harry Potter* book from my father as a birthday present. I was very surprised that my father gave me a book in English. "I want you to improve your English," my father said. From then on, I thought that if I wanted to understand the book in English, I needed to enrich my vocabulary. I began to copy the English dictionary. Every morning, I copied at least 30 words. Day after day, I found that I knew more words, and then I began to read *Harry Potter*. There were still lots of new words in the book when I read it for the first time. I checked in the dictionary for the words which I did not know and then copied them. Fortunately, I understood all the words when I read the book for the second time. As a Chinese student, I think that vocabulary is the foundation of learning English reading and writing. The structure of the sentences was also a problem to me. In order to address this problem, I tried to read more and practiced analyzing the structure of each sentence, especially the complex sentences. After practicing, I think I became better.

I really started my English journey about one month ago, when I started to study at CSUN. Everything was new to me. To be honest, I could not really understand what the professors said in class in the first week. My first class was English. After my first time writing an in-class essay, I felt very upset. I knew most of the words in the article, but I really did not understand the main idea of the article. So I wrote the essay without integrating the article. What a horrible essay I wrote! I asked my English teacher, Professor Anna Dawahare, to help me. She told me that there were going to be things in class that were very different from my culture and language. Professor Dawahare suggested to me that I needed some extra information in order to understand the cultural context of the things I read. I think this was a very good suggestion for me. When I read "Learning to Read," by Malcolm X, I tried to research the author's background before I started reading the article. This helped me to more easily understand the article.

I also read the article "Learning to Read and Write," by Frederick Douglass. The article was very meaningful to me. In this essay, Douglass tells the story of his coming to literacy, which reminds me of my own experience. I absolutely understand that literacy does not mean simply learning how to read or how to write. In my opinion, literacy is the ability to make some connections between our own experiences and the things we read. I understand the vocabulary in the things I read, but sometimes I do not understand the main ideas in the readings. I think the reason I cannot always understand the readings is that I do not know the background. It is culture shock that makes me confused. When I have some trouble in reading and understanding the things I read, isn't it necessary that I ask friends, especially foreign friends, for help? Douglass learned how to read by making friends of all the little white boys whom he met in the street and gave some bread so that he could obtain knowledge, which was more valuable than bread (119). I think this way is very useful. Since reading Douglass's essay, when I do not really understand the things I read, I try to ask my friend, a girl born in Los Angeles, some questions about the authors, the backgrounds, and so on. I can more easily understand the things I read by searching for more information on the cultural context of the reading.

On my English learning journey, I hope I can improve not only my reading skills but also my English writing skills; on the way to success, I want to know more about the world by reading.

Work Cited

Douglass, Frederick."Learning to Read and Write." *Fifty Essays: A Portable Anthology*. 4th ed. Ed. Samuel Cohen. Boston/New York: Bedford/St. Martin's, 2013. 118–123. Print.

> *Staring at the cover for a while, I felt an energy*
> *pulling me close to the book.*

Trang Nguyen

Instructor: Mary Marca

My Trouble with Reading

Most kids growing up will bond with the fantasy world of fairy tales. They dream about a happy ending with a charming prince or loving parents. My childhood started as sweet as any other childhood. I loved reading and living in the world of fairy tales.

I grew up in a warm and perfect family. I heard many times how proud my mom was when she saw me reading a small book at two years old. She always picked books with colorful images to excite me. I don't think I knew how to read at that time. My mom was the one who told me all the best bedtime stories. She also read books for me so I would sit still to eat. I liked how she acted like the characters in the books and made me laugh. That was how I remembered the stories. The next time I opened the book, I believed I could read it fluently, but I actually just recalled what my mom had read on each page and repeated her. That was the first time I appreciated and felt interested in reading.

At the age of four, I started learning how to read and understand stories. I read books anywhere, any time I could. My parents encouraged me to keep reading. On my birthday, I didn't want anything but books. Time passed, and I had such a big collection of books that, on my bookshelf, there wasn't enough space for my treasures; I had to stack them on the floor. I loved to read and dream about the worlds in those stories.

Everything seemed to be perfect until I got hit by a family issue. Fifth grade was a horrible time in my life. My parents had a cold war. They were angry with each other, but they never acted it out. Not long after the invisible chaos, my parents separated. I was ten years old, but I had to witness a lot of tears and pain from both my mom and my dad. Everything changed. I lived with my father who unintentionally poured his sadness over my head. Whenever he saw me reading, he would come and yell at me. He said that I was reading stupid stuff and all those books were a big lie. If happy endings existed like in those fairy tales, my parents would never have broken up. I started thinking that books were not as perfect as I had thought, so I refused to read and decided to grow up. At ten, I had to think like an adult. I sold all my books and emptied all the shelves without mercy. I hated reading so badly that I didn't touch any books, magazines, or even textbooks. Although my teachers yelled at me because I never read books for homework, I didn't care.

For six tough years I couldn't read properly, but when I finally got to high school, I met my savior—my best friend, Yen. She offered to be my friend and teach me how to read. She said straight to my face that my reading sucked. It was true; I couldn't pronounce a simple word correctly. She didn't give up on me; she didn't care what reasons I had to not read. She attacked me with everything she had to force me to read. She tricked me to go to the bookstore with her. Since I had no other friends, I went with her everywhere she wanted. Yen dragged me to every single bookstore in the city. We went so often so that the owners recognized our faces very well. Or maybe I thought they recognized us because we were the only ones who came to their bookstores and never bought one single book.

One day, Yen dragged me to a store that I had never been to before. Dream Books was quite big and neat, but old. I was very curious about the promotion that the store had in front of the door. On the big poster were the words: "Do you want to get a thrill?" in the color of blood and under those letters was the cover of the book *The Moonlight Project*, by Quy Co Nu. Looking at the squiggly lines on the cover, the bizarre moon on the top left, and the shadow of a person on the ground, I got goose bumps. I thought this would be a good book to read since I liked the horror genre. When I went inside, I was surprised by a huge table with stacks and stacks of the book that I had seen on the poster. Staring at the cover for a while, I felt an energy pulling me close to the book. Suddenly I picked one, went to a corner, and started reading. Yen followed me. That was the first time she had seen me reading, so she didn't want anyone to interrupt me. She watched the shopkeeper for me, so I could read. This might have been the best book I had ever read.

I guess I felt like Helen Keller, an incredible blind and deaf woman who tried to learn language for the first time in 1887. After going through lots of struggles, Keller finally could understand the meaning of a word when she first touched water: "Suddenly [she] felt a misty consciousness as of something forgotten—a thrill of returning thought; and somehow the mystery of language was revealed." Just like Keller, I felt that something I had abandoned had come back to me. Reading *The Moonlight Project* for a few pages made me remember how much I had loved reading, how many books I once had, and how I had mistreated what I once called "a treasure." I cried when I read it. I realized I had missed reading. The book had lured me into a different world, the world of horror and terror. The book brought me into its world to experience what Diep Hinh (the main character) had been through. Diep Hinh was the only one who could sense the strange things that others couldn't feel, so she had been swept into the vortex of horror.

Another trouble came to me: I didn't have money to buy the book. Neither I nor Yen had money to buy a proper book. To celebrate the old Trang coming back and to satisfy our coveted reading of that book, Yen and I sketched a crazy plan. We took turns to read every day, sometimes staying until the store closed. It was fun for me to read illegally. I learned to read fast, but capture everything in the book. We got caught many times because the store had cameras, but Yen and I didn't give up so easily; finally, the storekeeper didn't bother to watch us. Every time I had to stop reading, I was dying to know what would happen next. I loved how the author described the anatomy which Diep Hinh had to learn as a surgeon trainee in the book. I was crazy enough to study physiology because I wanted to experience this in real life. It changed my ideas of a career. I was crazy enough about that book to draw every single anatomy scene. After *The Moonlight Project*, I read a lot of detective and horror novels.

Thank you, Yen—a friend who brought me back to reading, and a friend who understood how a book could affect me. Yen reminded me how much I loved reading, and how wrong I was about the world of books. It is a world that rescues my soul from hate and sorrow. It is a world that helps me experience many adventurous journeys in my mind.

Works Cited

Keller, Helen. "The Most Important Day." *Models for Writers: Short Essays for Composition*. Eds. Alfred Rosa and Paul Eschholz. Boston/New York: Bedford/St.Martin's, 2012. 84–87. Print.

Quy Co Nu. *The Moonlight Project*. Vietnam: Ha Noi, 2005. Print. (In Vietnamese).

> *The fact that reading and writing meant so much to my parents made me like doing both. I didn't want them to think all those days and nights they spent with me were for nothing.*

MOISES NAVARRETE

Instructor: Mary Marca

MOM AND DAD

There are many relationships that I've had with friends, co-workers, and family that have helped me in my journey towards becoming a man; however, there is no one who can take my parents' place. My parents have shaped me into who I am today: a musician, an athlete, and a responsible person. If there's something they've always taught me to be, more than anything, it's a reader and a writer.

My parents come from very poor families who believed only in working, getting married, and working some more. My dad always wanted to learn how to be a great writer; unfortunately, that opportunity wasn't given to him as a young man. My mom took a keen interest in reading, but she didn't have school or anyone to teach her. She had to find ways to learn on her own. My parents never failed to remind me every day how important school was, and every time I came home from school, I was expected to read either the Bible or a newspaper for at least 10 minutes. I always found it annoying, but at the end of the day, I understood why they did it and why they were so passionate about my education.

The majority of my dad's side of the family are devoted musicians. Some play instruments, some sing, and some write poems and/or music; my dad did all three. He never forced me to do any of those things, but it would bring him joy when I would at least try. I wanted my dad to be just as proud of me as he was of my older brother, so I started writing music at a very early age; I was 10 years old when I wrote my first song. As I fell in love with music, I learned to fall in love with writing as well. The idea of being able to express myself was amazing; however, my writing wasn't always as it is today. My dad had to spend a lot of time with me on my school work when he would come home from work. Sometimes I felt like giving up, but my dad was always there to help me realize what my mistakes were, and thanks to that, I learned how to spot them when I make them.

My mom's side of the family was always strict, but they were all well mannered and respectful. My mom always made sure I was on top of my academics. There was no such thing as procrastinating when she was around. It was either do your homework, then watch TV, or don't watch TV at all. Although my mom was never taught how to read and write, she always made sure I made the best out of the opportunity to learn. There was a night that I had a disagreement with her because I didn't want to do my homework, but instead of punishing me that night, she decided to sit down with me and explain how important it is to read and write and how many opportunities she couldn't take because she didn't know how. I look back to that night every time I have a writing assignment and remind myself how important it is, not only for me, but for my mom as well.

I remember having to write on Nathaniel Hawthorne's novel *The Scarlet Letter*, a book that was nowhere near my taste in reading. I couldn't find a reason to actually read it, other than it being an assignment. I told my parents about my situation, and they thought of no better way to help me than not letting me go out with my friends until I had read the book and summarized it. I hated them for that at first, but when the final essay came around, I had all the summaries that my parents had made me do to help me out. Having strict parents had its cons, but the pros outweighed them in the long run.

I often had a hard time at school, but my parents were always there to try and pick me up. When there were nights I was stuck on a prompt, my dad would help me choose a route that I should take with my writing and he would stay there the whole night if he had to. My mom was always the one to stay up with me while I read. She wouldn't understand what I was reading, but regardless, she was always there to keep me company. The fact that reading and writing meant so much to my parents made me like doing both. I didn't want them to think all those days and nights they spent with me were for nothing.

Frederick Douglass, a slave from Talbot County, Maryland, is someone I can relate to. Douglass writes, "The plan which I adopted, and the one by which I was most successful, was that of making friends of all the little white boys whom I met in the street. As many of these as I could, I converted into teachers" (39). As a slave, it was impossible for Douglass to receive any education, but he had a desire to learn and that desire fueled him to do whatever it took to reach his goal. I used my parents as teachers and motivation for my reading and writing, just like he used the "little white boys." Although I didn't learn everything I know from my parents, as Douglass did with the kids, most of my writing style has evolved because of the things my dad taught me.

My parents' hard work and dedication towards my education has helped me tremendously so far in my college career. Without them, I don't believe my interest in reading, writing, or education would have been as strong as it is today. My goal is to keep making them proud by writing exceptional papers and keeping all of the lessons they've taught me alive and close to my heart.

Work Cited

Douglass, Frederick. "How I Learned to Read and Write." *The Norton Reader.* Eds. Linda Peterson, John Brereton, Joseph Bizup, Anne Fernald, Melissa Goldthwaite. New York: W.W. Norton & Company, 2012. 191–194. Print.

> *"I was prepared to talk with the girl of my dreams, but I blew it because I was too scared that I did not speak English as well as she did."*

Emanuel Moreno Valdez

Instructor: Masha Grigoryan

The Curious Beast: A Scene

After walking for hours on what seemed to be the black side of the moon, I found myself in a white room. In the distance, I could see someone inside a huge cage that seemed designed to contain a monster. As I approached the cage, I recognized a human form, probably a male. When I reached the cage, I could not believe my eyes—the person inside the cage was a 15-year-old version of myself! With confusion clouding my vision, I said, "I remember you."

He looked at me with the same confusion, for what felt like an eternity but was only a moment in real time, and asked, "Are you who I think you are?"

I smiled and said, "Yes; I used to be you."

We both laughed. I asked him if Uncle Mario had talked to him yet. The light-hearted laugh stopped and the smile disappeared, replaced by an expression of pain as he lowered his eyes and said hesitatingly, "He just did." He curled himself into the fetal position, crying. "I don't believe I can be what my whole family expects of me," he said. "Since you're an older version of me, you already know that Uncle Mario said that he does not believe in me."

"Yes, I know," I replied, remembering that conversation with Uncle Mario and all the hurt that had swelled up inside me afterward. "But he also said that he wanted you to prove him wrong!" I added. My younger self shot me a look of disbelief and fixated his stare, clearly processing a question in his mind.

"If you are me...how did I become you?" he asked, with a curious expression on his young, naive face.

I scratched the back of my neck and with a confident smile responded, "You become me because you prove Uncle Mario wrong."

At these words, he stood up and wiped his tears with a sleeve, his eyes opening so wide that I felt they were going to eat me up completely. Emanuel from 2011 continued to stare, but it was a contemplative stare, one that hid behind it the desire to understand, plan, and succeed. He looked at me long enough to realize that he would become the man he wanted to become. He asked, "How did I prove Uncle Mario wrong?"

I looked deep inside myself to find an answer that would satisfy the curious beast inside the cage, but the best thing I could come up with was, "You discovered that you were not alone; you found the only person on the planet with the key that could open that cage and set you free."

As I expected, my answer wasn't enough to satisfy the hunger for answers in his eyes. "But who is that person? Who is he or she?" he asked, confused by my response. Overtaken by excitement and the prospect of knowing something about his future, he kept badgering me for a reply without giving me a moment to insert a word. "Please! Tell me!"

I just looked at him and said, "Mom was right. We used to be annoying."

We broke out in simultaneous laughter. But our laughter was eventually washed over by a deep and heavy silence.

I said, "You know, even though Uncle Mario didn't believe in us, Mom, Dad, and even our siblings always believed in us. Of all the things that I had to learn in these four years, that was the fuel that kept me going." I was looking at the ground when I said this, but as I finished speaking, I could see Emanuel from 2011's face from the corner of my eye; it resembled the face of someone who had just made a major breakthrough, like a mathematician who had just solved the world's most complicated equation. His entire face yelled, "Eureka!"

He stayed silent for a few seconds and then said, "Uncle Mario was wrong. He didn't know me as well as my parents do!" Although he sounded a bit aggressive while saying this, he also seemed happy that he had figured it out. Or rather, that someone had helped him figure it out. I always dreamed of such an opportunity. I remember being him and hoping someone would tell me, help me, guide me. Seeing him glow with confidence and joy at the idea that he would grow up to be happy and successful made me smile.

I looked at Emanuel from 2011 and said, "The first step you should take is to join the Cross Country team, and there you will find the key that will break you out."

As if this had been an order given from God, he replied, "I will do it as fast as I can."

I smiled at his youthful vigor and the ease with which he made decisions. Having the power to influence him also made me happy and I said, "You should also try to practice your English more. Although it seems impossible to learn, you will learn it, but a little more practice won't hurt."

Emanuel from 2011 looked at me and asked, "Do you have any regrets?"

Thoughts flooded my mind—dozens of moments of embarrassment, little and big. However, the only moment of regret that I could think of was when I failed to tell the girl I loved that I loved her.

The Curious Beast: A Scene

"There is only one time I regret," I began. "It happened one night at a party where I was prepared to talk with the girl of my dreams, but I blew it because I was too scared that I did not speak English as well as she did."

"What happened after that?"

"I decided to study extra hard to learn English so that I could talk to her. But even though I learned enough, I lacked the courage to do it. While I regret not talking to her, the desire to speak to her motivated me to improve my English, which let me graduate with honors from my high school."

Emanuel from 2011 looked at me and said with a wink, "Don't worry, I won't let that happen again."

Suddenly, I heard a sound in the distance and my whole body started drifting away from the cage. The sound got louder and louder, forcing me to cover my ears from its invasive noise. The last thing I saw was the cage disappear, and as it vanished I heard a whisper, "You set me free…"

I open my eyes and turn off my alarm.

ASSIGNMENTS

What Does the Writer Say?

1. What circumstances led the authors in this section to improve themselves as readers and writers? What specific reading and writing strategies do they identify as helpful?

2. What does each author believe is the value of learning to read and write? Compare and contrast the different ways in which the individual authors describe the personal importance of reading and writing.

What Do You Say?

3. Each author names a person or group of people who have contributed to his or her individual journey to literacy. For authors Jing Huang and Moises Navarrete, professors and parents had a positive influence on their learning experiences, while for authors Emanuel Valdez and Trang Nguyen, parents and relatives can sometimes create a more negative learning experience. Identify a person or group of people who made an impact on your path toward literacy in a positive or negative way. Describe what they did.

4. In Emanuel Valdez's narrative "The Curious Beast," the author uses descriptive language and dialogue to captivate readers and to help readers visualize the conversation between his 2011 self and his present-day self. Use descriptive language and dialogue to write a conversation between yourself now and an earlier version of yourself. What message would you convey?

Writing Exercises

5. For this exercise, write a 1–2 page narrative in which you respond to the following:

   In his essay, "Mom and Dad," Moises Navarrete explains, "As I fell in love with music, I learned to fall in love with writing as well. The idea of being able to express myself was amazing." What activities or hobbies do you immerse yourself in or are you passionate about? How do your interests compare to the act of writing?

6. For this exercise, write a 1–2 page narrative in which you respond to the following:

   In Trang Nguyen's essay "My Trouble with Reading," Nguyen learns how the act of reading "rescues [the] soul from hate and sorrow. It is a world that helps me experience many adventurous journeys in my mind." Describe how your reading experience compares to or differs from the experience that Nguyen describes.

Notes, Responses, & Ideas

SECTION 2:
VALUING EDUCATION

QUICK WRITE:

How do you learn best? By reading? Listening? Doing? Describe your most enjoyable and most unpleasant learning experiences.

NOTES, RESPONSES, & IDEAS

...good education saves lives and encourages the future.

CATALINA ROLDAN

Instructor: Amy Reynolds

SUMMARY/RESPONSE/LETTER: 3 EXERCISES BASED ON LYNDA BARRY'S "SANCTUARY"

SUMMARY

Lynda Barry's narrative, "Sanctuary," is a collection of her childhood memories of elementary school. Barry reveals that she grew up in an unstable home and describes how unnoticed she felt in her household. One time, she woke up with the immense desire to rush to school. She waited on the play-field until she was acknowledged by Mr. Gunderson, the janitor, who allowed her to come along with him to open the school and start the day. While help-ing him, Barry sees Mrs. Holman and Mr. Cunningham, who waved at her. Subsequently, she saw Mrs. LeSane, who walked towards her and greeted her gladly. Barry unexpectedly ran towards her, crying. She recalls her reaction as a moment of relief and belonging. Mrs. LeSane asked if she wanted to draw a picture. Barry later explains that drawing became "a life preserver" for her. Yet the government limits the budget for public schools, salaries for teachers, creative activities, and after-school programs in a world where good education saves lives and encourages the future.

RESPONSE

I can relate to Barry's love and gratitude towards her teachers and school. In the summer of 2010, I was accepted by lottery enrollment to HTLA High School, and my world flipped 360 degrees—in a positive way. The best part was the teachers and administrators, who were caring and understand-ing. HTLA's teachers not only helped with my English skills, but they also believed in me and gave me confidence to keep pushing forward through as-signments that were difficult. At the end of ninth grade, my teachers nominat-ed me as one of HTLA's Ambassadors, which was an honor because I helped prospective parents and students learn all about our school. I strongly believe in education and the power of creative activities. I proudly join Berry and hope for "our country to face its children and say the Pledge of Allegiance back."

19

LETTER

Dear Mrs. Oliveri,

I would like to thank you for taking time out of your busy life to be my interviewee. It was more than a pleasure to learn about your perspective towards education and hear your great story about advocating for adult education at the West Valley Occupational Center. I found it very interesting that we both share similar views on education: for example, the fact that education is a blessing and it should be something we are excited for. I also can see how easy it is for students who live in the United States. They already know the language, English, and because they are citizens, they can take advantage of financial aid.

In my English class, we have discussed so many different perspectives and stories about education, but the one that catches my attention the most is that attending a university truly isn't for everybody. As you said, everyone has different abilities or capacities for learning. In my case, I love hands-on learning. I think it's how I really learn because I get to think, and at the same time, take action. You might have heard about Fredrick Douglass, an honorable and exemplary soul who learned how to read and write by himself in the midst of slavery and conflict with his owners. He is an example of someone who acquired knowledge without going to school.

On the other hand, Lynda Barry fell in love with school at a young age. She valued going to school because she felt heard and noticed by her teachers. I can surely understand why she loved going to school. When I was in high school, I was the same way. I believe that teachers sometimes can be more encouraging than parents because they are almost parental figures without being too parental. They aren't as closed minded about certain things.

Today, something really interesting came up in a group discussion regarding education at a 'late age' or, in other words, adult education. We all agreed that it isn't ever too late to attend school, and I immediately thought about you fighting LAUSD so they wouldn't close the school you went to with many other adults looking for better opportunities. Thank you for that incredible gesture towards education. You are truly inspiring. Once again, thank you so much for letting me learn about your experiences and views. It was an honor.

Sincerely,
Catalina
PS: I think we should have another cup of coffee and discuss other subjects.

> *...my teachers did not bother to help me. Instead,*
> *they beat me and made me feel stupid.*

MUDDASSIR BILLOO
Instructor: Amy Reynolds

APPRECIATING EDUCATION: ESSAY INSPIRED BY LYNDA BARRY'S "SANCTUARY"

Education is valued more in undeveloped nations, where pursuing education is difficult, compared to the developed nations where education is free. Education is the key to success and this success should not be taken for granted. People value education in undeveloped nations because their countries do not provide support for education and they have limited educational rights, unlike American students who take education for granted despite having free access to public schools.

Pakistan, where I was born, provides very limited access to education. For example, when I was in middle school in Pakistan, my family had to pay for the school's tuition. When I was in eighth grade, my parents were stuck in a financial crisis which affected my enrollment status. I cried in front of my middle school's principal to not expel me, but he refused to listen to me and forced me to leave. Before my expulsion, education was my only option for socialization, because at home, I felt sad to see my parents fighting every day. By going to school, I was able to learn and make my day productive, rather than being depressed at home.

I remember that when I received my expulsion certificate, I went to many houses of my family and knocked for help, but unfortunately, no one was willing to help me. I waited for almost three months until my dad finally got design contracts as an engineer. However, even after my dad's return to financial stability, he refused to help me with my education, and instead, encouraged me to join his construction team. I refused his suggestion and appealed to my mother, who sold her gold and re-enrolled me in middle school to satisfy my need for education.

APPRECIATING EDUCATION: ESSAY INSPIRED BY LYNDA BARRY'S "SANCTUARY"

When I finally returned to school, I saw that the whole school was preparing for final exams. When I went to ask my teachers for help, instead of helping, they slapped me and threw chalk at me, despite knowing my reason for three months of absence. My best friends became mean and did not help. I was all alone, surrounded by four walls. I did not know how to begin demolishing the walls that were trapping me behind my peers and keeping me from successfully finishing the term and getting into high school. Seeking help from my brother and sister and using an American website, Purple Math, allowed me to understand the material. During final test days, the electric supply was short in the whole city; therefore, I had to study by candlelight on my terrace and endure Pakistan's intense heat at night. Not only did I study without lights or fans, but I also took final examinations at school without electricity.

American students are lucky because they live with chilled air conditioning to take away the annoying heat, and in the winter, they have a warm furnace which takes away ice-cold weather. When I remember enduring difficulties in Pakistan for not being able to attend school for free, it makes me sad to see Americans who have access to quality education take it for granted, and do not push themselves to benefit from free public schooling.

I see a similar experience in the story "Sanctuary," by Lynda Barry. In this story, the narrator suffers from her parents' continuous fights at home. She sneaks out of her house early to spend time at school. She enjoys being at school because everyone respects her and embraces her. Reading "Sanctuary" allowed me to realize that the narrator was lucky because she had teachers who actually cared for her, while my teachers did not bother to help me. Instead, they beat me and made me feel stupid. However, even after my teachers' abusive behavior, I respected them until the end and never raised my voice to stop them because I was always taught to respect people who supply knowledge.

Many students in developed nations such as the United States take education for granted. For example, I saw a classmate in a high-school English class tearing California state exams into pieces and throwing them in my teacher's face. I shed tears when I saw the student's attitude toward my teacher. In Islam, respecting a teacher who shares knowledge with others is mandatory and I was taught this throughout my middle school in Pakistan. When my classmate threw the state test at my English teacher's face, I felt it was very unethical. My classmate ruined his future success by not taking education seriously and being expelled from high school.

I had to endure hardships upon entering a United States high school and I had to overcome countless obstacles to learn English. I may not have had to endure these struggles if I had been born in a developed country like the

United States. Although I feel bad for not getting into a single-semester college English class, I still appreciate my high-school English teachers because they gave up their lunch time to help me write essays. Due to my teachers' generous help in high school, I was able to start my college classes productively.

Attending an American high school and an American university makes me feel blessed. Here, in the United States, school administrators understand difficulties and grant extensions to students to help them pay tuition later. It is so different seeing how much the government of the United States cares for education, while in Pakistan, the government does not care about what happens to the education system. Pursuing education in the United States is not as tough as it is in Pakistan because everyone in this nation wants to help you reach your highest potential.

In the essay "Valuing Education," Sara Richards says, "Many students in America do not take the time to appreciate how lucky they are when it comes to receiving free education. Americans think that they have it hard and often complain about hating school, but there are those on the other side of the world who would love to take our spots in the classroom" (41). American students do not appreciate school because they are granted this resource from birth. American-style education in Pakistan costs about $13,896, more than CSUN's annual tuition. In fact, in the United States no student of K-12 standing is asked to pay for tuition. Even after this huge privilege, many American students hate high school and are often absent just to get their sleep.

Looking from both the blind and the bright sides of the world motivates me to achieve more in the United States because of the hardships that I endured in Pakistan. Whenever I feel weak and overwhelmed by my schoolwork, I always recall my situation when I was in middle school, taking exams while constantly sweating without the privilege of lights or an air-conditioner. My experience in Pakistan awakens me to achieve, and seeing poor students in Pakistan begging for food motivates me to fully take advantage of American resources to open the door of success.

According to UNESCO, Pakistan has the world's second highest number of children out of school, reaching 8.3 million in 2012—equivalent to 1 in 12 of the world's out-of-school children (CNN). Seeing these statistics really makes me feel bad about the future of Pakistan. If we compare these vulnerable kids to American kids, there is no doubt that Americans not only have good education but also have human rights to protect them from the brutal acts that Pakistani children often endure.

Besides Pakistan, there are many other nations on this planet where education is tough to pursue. Interviewing my high-school friend, Manny, allowed me to realize that some strong people in Mexico put their lives at risk to cross the border to enter the United States. I found that my friend had to work hard in Mexico to survive. He also had similar thoughts about Americans' attitudes toward education. He also believes that Americans should respect and take full advantage of public-school resources, rather than complaining and not finishing.

Having a negative experience in a third-world country and a positive experience in a developed nation gives me the endurance to achieve and appreciate what advantages I possess. I tend to appreciate the United States' opportunities more than some of my friends because I craved these opportunities in Pakistan. Today, I am studying in one of America's well-known business schools because I stood strong and faced all the hardships. If people come to know more about the thirst for education around the globe, especially in Pakistan, then perhaps this may drive them to reach their highest potential.

Works Cited

Andrade, Manny. Personal Interview. 13 Sept. 2014.

Barry, Lynda. "Sanctuary." *Baltimore Sun*, 24 Jan. 1992. Print.

"Pakistan's Educational Challenges." *CNN*. Cable News Network, Web. 04 Nov. 2014

Richards, Sara. *New Voices*. Eds. Sandra Jackson and Amy Reynolds. Ed. 24. Northridge: Hayden McNeil, 2014. Print.

> *"There are people out there who have it way easier than you do,*
> *and don't take a single step to advancing their education."*

DIANNA ZARAGOZA

Instructor: Keli Rowley

THE NURSE WHO CHANGED MY LIFE

I grew up practically raising myself. When I was young, my mother worked day and night to provide a home for my three siblings and me. My father never really helped out with child support, so my mom spent six out of seven days a week working two jobs. One day, my mother met a man who satisfied her life in every aspect. Little did I know that she would be moving away, and I would be staying with my not-so-responsible father. My father is a fifty-four year old construction worker who thinks he's twenty-two and doesn't even make minimum wage. As a result, throughout high school, I struggled in pretty much every facet of my life. In senior year, I was a teacher's assistant in the health office, somewhere I felt at home. As the year progressed, I would meet the most positive influence in my life.

Melinda Jacobson, the school nurse, was a tall, skinny, independent, hard-working woman in her fifties who looked and acted like she was in her mid-thirties. She gave me "tough love." If I was wrong about something, she would correct me, and if I was correct, she would give me credit. One day, she asked me to translate for a student's mother who spoke only Spanish. The mother was wondering why her son was not allowed to wear his knee brace on school grounds. Ms. Jacobsen asked me to translate word for word, which I did. The parents were highly upset that their son needed a doctor's note in order to wear his brace on school grounds; apparently, they had no health insurance. Ms. Jacobson began explaining to me that it was very important they received the correct information; she said that policies were strict and that the LAUSD required all nurses to give exact information of the student's visit to the health office. I knew right off the bat that this woman was dedicated to her job.

Although she was a very busy woman, Ms. Jacobson found a way to make time for me. In my senior year, I wasn't financially stable enough to participate in any of my senior activities, but she made sure I didn't miss out. I remember it was the day before the weekend of homecoming, and also my birthday, when I was summoned to the health office. Ms. Jacobson handed me an envelope that said, "Happy Birthday." At this point I thought it was a gift card. She was persistent and made sure I opened it in front of her. As I opened the envelope, my heart started pounding: it was the last entrance ticket to homecoming. I was so ecstatic that I was going to celebrate homecoming the day before my birthday. The day of homecoming started with my "beautification," while the night was amazing and definitely a story to remember.

I walked into the health office on the Monday morning after homecoming to thank Ms. Jacobson for the ticket, but all the lights were off. On my desk, I saw a cake with my name and "Happy Birthday" written on it. As soon as I sat down, everyone from the attendance office, health office, and dean's office walked in, singing "Happy Birthday." My face lit up and I blushed bright red. After I served and ate cake, Ms. Jacobson sat down next to me and shared private information that was close to her heart, which enabled me to trust her and grow closer to her. Later, Ms. Jacobson also surprised me with free prom and grad-night tickets, and managed to get her hands on a yearbook for me.

The assistant principal encouraged me to apply for a scholarship that required a five-hundred word essay describing my accomplishments and what made me want to go to college. After finishing the essay, I realized I needed it proofread, so I asked Ms. Jacobson if she could read it over for me. About two days later, I was summoned to the health office. I was worried that I hadn't properly filed a medical form the day before.

As I walked into the nurse's office, Ms. Jacobson stood there with her arms wide open. As she hugged me, she said, "Honey, I am so proud of you. There are people out there that have it way easier than you do and don't take a single step to advancing their education. You are always smiling and always so helpful in the office. I'm glad you allowed me to proofread your essay." She handed it back to me with a paper attached, mentioning things I needed to fix and also a note saying, "Never give up; keep dreaming." As I began to shed my first tear, she told me that whatever I was going through helped to shape the strong woman I was becoming.

Ms. Jacobsen changed me in inexplicable ways. She made my senior year a memorable experience in that she taught me how to balance my personal life with my school life. She made me realize that everyone goes through their struggles differently. She has been a friend, mother figure, and someone I can trust with my life. I don't know where I would be if I hadn't met her. To this day we still talk; she called me about a month ago and we went out for dinner. When she realized I was still going through a difficult situation, she offered me her home to live in. I didn't move in with her, but I appreciated the offer. Who knew that my high-school nurse was going to change my life completely? She showed me that I am worthy of success.

> *College is not all fun and games; it's hard work and lots of willpower.*

Angela Pham
Instructor: Mahta Rosenfeld

A Day in the Life of a CSUN Student

Buzz…Bzzzz.…Bzzzz. My phone vibrates on the silver table in Bayramian Hall. It's so warm in here, with a light, clean scent in the air. I had dozed off, until my boyfriend, Johnmichael, abruptly texted me: "Awake Bebe!? Morning! Rise and Shine! MUAH<3."

I text him back, "Morning Bebe! Awww, I Love You! MUAH<3." It's 7:30 a.m. I stretch out my body to wake myself up, extending my hands as high as I can. If it were up to me, I would much rather be home asleep in my comfy warm bed; however, my loving mother drops me off at Bayramian Hall every day at 7am. *Now it's time to work!* Looking around me, I'm happy to see that there are fewer people here. I look in my large, black JanSport backpack; hesitantly, I pull out my black Mac Pro Laptop (I chose this color to match my daily outfits). I know I need to start homework; however, I would rather watch YouTube videos till class instead. *Bzzzz. Bzzzz.* I receive another text, "Muah! Muah! Bebe, what are you doing?"

I reply, "On my laptop about to study biology." Staring at my laptop screen, I study the human body. I occasionally glance down at my colorful keyboard that looks like an ombre rainbow river.

Alexis, my friend of three years, comes through the front door of Bayramian Hall; I wave to her. She is my curly-haired, light-skinned, five-foot-two Latina girlfriend. She struts up to me, all smiling with her deep, hollow dimples. Standing in front of me she says, "Hey, Angela! Ready to go?"

Smiling back I say, "Hey, Alexis! Yeah!" Putting everything inside my JanSport, I zip it up and extend my arms into both thick black straps. Plopping it on my back, it yanks my shoulders downward: my black anchor. We both head to our favorite "secret spot" in the Oviatt Library. It's not really a secret location, but it's in a dim corner of the library. In these booths, I feel as if I'm in my own personal bubble.

A Day in the Life of a CSUN Student

The day flies by so fast as I study biology; I look at the time and it's noon. I dash to my Biology 101 class in Eucalyptus Hall. I love sitting in the front, and because it's such a large class, I have to rush in early to get a good seat. I enter my favorite class of the day and take a seat in front of the professor's podium. I also save a seat on my right for my other Latina girlfriend, Lidia, who always comes to class right as the professor is ready to lecture. I check my text from Johnmichael, "Alright Bebe have fun in your classes! Study hard and txt me when ur days over!" *Aww...I love him! He's right. Now it's education time! No time to waste!*

Lidia rushes through the door; out of breath and smiling at me, she says, "Aww, thank you, Angela. Did I miss anything?"

I smile back to tell her, "No problem, Hun. And no, he's about to start."

As Professor E. lectures, I listen in and take key notes on everything he says. I absolutely love when he says the words, "This may be on the test..." *On the TEST!* But sometimes, when I miss something, I turn to tap on Lidia's shoulder, and of course, she always helps me out. Honestly, without Lidia, biology wouldn't be as fun for me. We're partners: we share notes, study together, and rely on one another. My petite brunette is one of the smartest students in the class. She's always the only one asking questions and making comments, which makes it so much more interesting, while I'm avidly engaged in the lecture.

I'm a health administration major and naturally I am fascinated with science. Learning about the human body, what we are composed of, and how life is possible scientifically, interests me. I understand the material and am driven to know more, which is why I spend most of my days and nights studying biology. This leaves me with less time to study Math 104: Statistics. This is the class I'm struggling in dreadfully. I hear all through campus, "Do not take biology with statistics!" *Guess I didn't get the message early enough.*

I head to Chaparral Hall, the largest class of my evening, excited about the day almost coming to an end. With the same routine in all my classes, I sit near the front, facing the professor. I could be recognized; *it's very important for the teachers to see that students are trying and caring to do well in their classes.* I sit in seat D106, in the third of seven rows in class. I sit between both my close female friends: on my right, I have my voluminously curly-haired brunette, Curine, and on my left, I have my petite, bubbly, straight-black-haired Vanessa. Together we are the math trio, always helping one another out, studying consistently every other day of the week, and gossiping about our relationships. As Professor Z. starts the lecture, Vanessa determinedly tells me, "I'm gonna pay attention!"

I laugh back and turn my head to tell her, "We'll see…but alright, Hun."

I knew it. Here she is again, sleeping on my left shoulder. I would love to sleep too, but I know my priority is to focus on statistics. *Thank God! The professor makes jokes to crack me up or else I'd be napping as well.* Meanwhile, Curine and I take notes and share anything we miss. Occasionally, I glance at my phone to see the time, knowing in just a few more minutes, my lectures are done. As I jot down the last notes, Professor Z. says, "Alright everyone, have a nice evening." So thrilled the day's over, yet exhausted from it, I text Johnmichael: "Hey, Bebe! I'm done!"

I walk to the Orange Grove on campus to lie on a bench near the duck pond. Here I rest my head to look up at the sky. *College is not all fun and games; it's hard work and lots of willpower. Being a Health Administration major and trying to do my prerequisites for the BSN is very stressful. This is my life, my future, and my job in my own hands. I love science, English, and art, but that doesn't mean I'm great at math or foreign languages. I always tell myself, 'No one's perfect!'* This drives me to keep on trying, no matter the cost. Since I pay full tuition at California State University, Northridge, every cent reminds me to push to my limits, to not waste time, and to finish in four years if possible. What I do now will determine my future career.

Bzzz. Bzzz. I reach in my pocket to pull out my phone. He messages: "Awesome, Bebe! What now?"

I reply, "Now? It's time to study!"

Bzzz. Bzzz.

Assignments

What Does the Writer Say?

1. In "Appreciating Education," Muddassir Billoo supports his position on the state of education in America in different ways. What is Billoo's position? What different types of supporting evidence does he use?

2. What is the importance of education for each of the four authors in this section? If all four authors were sitting in a room together and discussing education, on what points would they agree? On what points would they disagree?

What Do You Say?

3. In "The Nurse Who Changed My Life," author Dianna Zaragoza identifies the school nurse as being someone who most positively influenced her educational journey. Name someone who extended kindness towards you in an unexpected way. Describe how their act of generosity helped you.

4. Identify the various pieces of advice that Angela Pham provides for college students in her essay, "A Day in the Life of a CSUN Student." What advice did you receive when you began college? Given your experience in college so far, which piece of advice seems most important for you to remember right now?

Writing Exercises

5. For this exercise, create a reverse outline for Catalina Roldan's letter to Gloria Oliveri. To do this, you will need to identify the main idea of each paragraph in a few brief words (no more than one full sentence). After completing the reverse outline, address the following questions: Why does Roldan choose to organize her paragraphs in that particular order? Would you have structured your letter to Mrs. Oliveri in a different way? Why or why not?

6. For this exercise, write a 1–2 page response to the following:

   Muddassir Billoo, author of "Appreciating Education," believes that people in America often take "education...for granted" and that they do "not push themselves to benefit from free public schooling." To what extent do you agree with Billoo? Use examples to support your position.

Karin Hildebrand Lau / Shutterstock.com

SECTION 3:
ANALYZING GENDER

QUICK WRITE:

Have you ever experienced or witnessed discrimination or stereo-typing? How did you react? How did that experience impact your life?

NOTES, RESPONSES, & IDEAS

There does not seem to be room for a boy to be nurturing and caring.

Susan Guthier

Instructor: Keli Rowley

Toys and Gender in Advertising

Upon learning your friend is pregnant, the first question that may come to mind is, "Do you know what you're having?" This is asked in order to purchase the right gift. And what is the right gift? The present should be cute and practical, but most importantly, it should scream the gender of the child: blue if it is a boy, and frilly pink if it's a girl. Toys often reinforce the child's gender role in society. Many times, boys are told to play only with tools, blocks, and trucks, while girls are pushed toward cooking utensils, dolls, and anything that is pink. Toy companies tailor their commercials to let kids know how they should act in our society. Parents further reinforce this as they control the funds and decide what to ultimately purchase for their children. Although toy ads that exploit gender are popular, they limit the possibilities of what kids are allowed to do. Instead, toy commercials should let kids be kids and not influence them to play only with toys that are connected to their gender.

Toy commercials are entertaining, but the underlying messages can be dangerous. In one commercial, we have boys between the ages of 8–10 playing with Marvel Comics accessories. More specifically, they are playing with "Hulk Hands," hands that you slip on like gloves and use to punch things around the house. The ad shows boys engaged in pretend fighting with each other. At first glance, this looks like a nice commercial showcasing a product based on a popular comic-book character. The commercial implies that if boys purchase these hands, they will possess the power of the comic-book superhero. However, this is problematic because no girls are featured in the commercial. Instead, all that is featured are boys, further insinuating that these toys are made only for boys' entertainment. In the article, "Are Gender Specific Toys Beneficial or Sexist?" journalist K.M. O'Sullivan says, "There is no such thing as a 'gender specific toy,' only gender-specific marketing within a culture that has, with very few exceptions, been conditioned to believe ads that continue to perpetuate the idea that girls will be girls and boys will be boys" (qtd in Breen). This supports the notion that the marketing machines would have you think the Hulk Hands are made for a boy. How? By showcasing actions, music, and colors that research says boys find more appealing.

Toys and Gender in Advertising

It is no secret that commercials geared toward boys illustrate them as having power and getting to destroy things. Boys are often relegated to the role of soldier or "protector." Take, for example, another commercial geared toward the male gender. In the "Man of Steel" commercial, boys are shown playing with a Superman toy with stretchy arms. The boys in the commercial are able to catapult Superman using his arms to attack his "enemies." Dramatic music plays in the background as key phrases such as "save the planet," "save the day," "help protect," and "take him out" are echoed all through the commercial. According to "Toy Ads and Learning Gender," Anita Sarkeesian, a media critic, says that commercials geared toward boys often showcase the following qualities: "competition, being in control, having power, and conquering and commanding." This commercial illustrates these qualities vividly as we see the boys taking on those roles—to help Superman save the planet, of course. Girls could have a role in this type of commercial by being shown playing with female superheroes doing the same kinds of activities.

But not all hope is lost. Society as a whole is becoming more conscious of what are being coined "gendered advertisements." There is a company called GoldieBlox that markets toys for girls, but the twist is the message that these commercials are disseminating: girls can build things, too. The commercial "GoldieBlox & Rube Goldberg" starts off with three girls watching a boring commercial about dancing and being a "pretty girl." The girls indicate they are bored, by their yawns. Suddenly, the music in the background changes to an uplifting and fun beat and so does the mood. The girls stand up and participate in what looks like creating and building an obstacle maze. At the end of the commercial, the screen fades out to showcase a multitude of products with the following message splashed on the side of the screen: "Toys for Future Engineers." This commercial has such a fresh take on toy advertising that is geared toward girls. The commercial does its best not to confine girls to the traditional roles of nurturer and caretaker. Instead, it is encouraging them to find science and math interesting as well.

If boys are constantly being bombarded with characteristics of dominance, power, and conquest in commercials, advertisers are reinforcing the notion that this is what is expected of them in real life. There does not seem to be room for a boy to be nurturing and caring (Sarkeesian). The characteristics of being nurturing and caring will be found in toy advertisements geared mainly toward girls. So how do we combat gender-specific toy advertisements? Writer Sarah Buttenwieser puts it best: "This seems to be the key with the gender-specific toys decision. Be mindful of what you purchase, offer a variety of choices, and then see what your child is drawn to. And then, let go. The play decision is ultimately theirs." In my opinion, this is the way all toy commercials should be made.

Works Cited

Breen, Galit. "Are Gender Specific Toys Beneficial Or Sexist?" *My Family.* She-knows Media, 2 Dec. 2003. Web. 13 Oct. 2014.

Fevolpe, "Incredible Hulk Hands Toy Commercial." Online video clip. *You-Tube*, 14 Oct. 2014. Web. 13 Oct. 2014.

GoldieBlox. "GoldieBlox & Rube Goldberg, Princess Machine." Online Video Clip. *YouTube*, 26 Nov. 2013. Web. 13 Oct. 2014.

Sarkeesian, Anita. "Toy Ads and Learning Gender." *FeministFrequency*, 16 Nov. 2010. Web. 13 Oct. 2014.

Younis, Steve. "Man of Steel Toy Commercial-Exploders." Online video clip. *YouTube*, 16 Oct. 2012. Web. 13 Oct. 2014.

With the emergence of culturally diverse princesses, Disney has positively influenced young children all over the globe...

LILIANA VALERIO

Instructor: Emily Olson

DISNEY PRINCESSES AS POSITIVE ROLE MODELS

Disney movies, especially the fairy tales, have been touching the lives of millions of people around the globe ever since the 1930s. From the very first princess, Snow White (1937), to the most current, Anna and Elsa (2013), one can only imagine how influential each princess has been on girls both young and old and society as a whole. Many of the films teach girls all over the world to show no fear in being who they are. Disney films also give young girls a positive influence on how to be courageous when tackling social challenges. Although some may argue that Disney provides girls with unrealistic romance ideals and negative gender roles, the beloved films provide many examples of positivity through love lessons, gender equality, and cultural diversity.

Thesis

Many people believe that Disney films are very unrealistic in depicting relationships, gender roles, and stereotypes. For example, Goal A. Saedi, of *Psychology Today*, critiques Disney's efforts by stating that "the fairy tale image is in many ways misleading, creating false expectations, and in essence, ruining modern day romance" (par. 6). However, taking a closer look at each film reveals the positive messages hidden in each tale. In each Disney princess movie, one can find a positive outlook on life for a young girl. For example, Jelani Addams Rosa, of *Seventeen* magazine, reminds Disney lovers and critics that Disney's fairy tale storylines actually teach people important lessons about love. She mentions the different lesson seen in each Disney movie: "don't fall too fast" in *Frozen*, "don't limit yourself to a certain 'type'" in *Aladdin*, "be yourself" in *The Little Mermaid*, "you have to give relationships room to grow" in Beauty and the Beast, "don't try to be someone you're not" in *Cinderella*, "honesty is the best policy" in *Mulan*, "sometimes love doesn't last forever" in *Pocahontas*, "never forget your friends" in *Snow White*, and "create your own happiness" in *The Princess and the Frog*. Rosa agrees that in these films, girls and teenagers are taught to love themselves and to stay true to who they are instead of changing their personalities just to be loved by someone else. Tiana, from *The Princess and the Frog*, shows girls that happiness does not always lie within the arms of a man and encourages girls to become strong, independent women, find their own dreams, and work hard to achieve them, therefore encouraging gender equality. However, perhaps a much better example of gender equality in Disney fairy tales is Mulan, who demonstrates that women are just as capable as men of doing hard labor, rather than sitting at home waiting for someone to provide for them. In *Aladdin*, girls are taught to be open to different cultures, not just through the love between Jasmine and Aladdin, but also through the different styles in clothing and appearance throughout the movie. The films also depict realistic encounters that young girls might face with love. For example, in the movie *Pocahontas*, the relationship between John Smith and Pocahontas does not end with them being together forever, giving girls the message that one's first relationship does not always end happily. Many of Disney's princesses send girls all over the world realistic messages about life and society.

While many may believe that Disney films provide young girls with unrealistic love images, modern Disney films have been shifting away from the traditional love between a man and woman to that of the love between family, friends, and the self. In her article, Saedi states that recent Disney films are "inching closer to stories that weave magic and love with more profound concepts such as inner strength and courage" (par. 12). For example, in the modern film *Brave*, Merida turns her mother into a bear while trying to prove herself worthy of ruling her family's kingdom without a man. On her journey to break the curse placed on her mother by a witch, Merida feels hopeless at first, but breaks the curse with the love she has for her mother. Through this newfound love between mother and daughter, young girls are taught that love can work its way through the struggles they face in the family. Another positive love lesson is seen in Disney's most recent princess film, *Frozen*. In the film, Anna does her best to assure her sister, Elsa, of the love she has for her but ends up getting struck by her sister's powers and is frozen to death. Just when viewers think that Anna's true love will break the frozen curse, it is Elsa's love for Anna that breaks the spell, teaching young girls that love can heal the wounds and resolve the conflicts within the family. Disney is encouraging young girls to see that the power of love keeps relationships strong.

Disney's influence on girls around the globe does not end with positive messages about love; it continues through the many depictions of gender equality. Many studies suggest that children's behavior is greatly influenced by the media. In an effort to reflect changing gender roles, Disney has deviated greatly from its previous view of women being domesticated, to one where women are independent, therefore creating a sense of gender equality. Bridget Whelan agrees when she describes how "*The Princess and the Frog* became the first Disney Princess film to feature a heroine who aspired for something more than romance throughout the film's narrative" (30). With dreams of opening her own restaurant, Princess Tiana was the first modern princess to teach young girls that having aspirations of becoming superior was not something to be sanctioned, and instead encouraged them to have big dreams of establishing themselves in society. Other modern fairy tales inspiring this very same message include *Brave*, where Merida teaches her parents that she can, in fact, take the throne without a man by her side; *Frozen*, where Elsa is queen of Erindale and rules the kingdom as well; and *Beauty and the Beast*, where Belle loves to read and learn. These films provide young girls with the positive message that it is acceptable to deviate from the traditional and stereotypical roles and establish themselves in society as who they wish to be.

Another positive influence on young girls within the spectrum of Disney fairy tales is the portrayal of cultural diversity. With the emergence of culturally diverse princesses, Disney has positively influenced young children all over the globe to feel that their culture is appreciated. In her article, Ashley Bispo notes that "the inclusion of different races in Disney films helps to convey the importance of other cultures to young viewers" (11). Bispo acknowledges Disney's effort to include diverse cultures through films such as *Mulan*, which depicts Chinese culture; *Aladdin*, depicting Arab culture; *Pocahontas*, which depicts American Indian culture; *The Princess and the Frog*, African American culture; *Brave*, Scottish culture; and *Frozen*, which characterizes Norwegian culture. Disney's involvement with culture shows that, as American society is more accepting of diversity through the emergence of the "melting pot," Disney films are reflecting that acceptance. With culturally diverse fairy tales available for Disney's young audience, children will be better able to connect to people of different cultures, as well as learn about culture in general.

While many will argue that Disney princesses provide young children with false and unrealistic representations of the world around them, the fairy tales do an exceptional job of being positive in many ways. Through representing love lessons, gender equality, and cultural diversity, Disney is creating a positive outlook on life for young children around the globe, and that effort should be recognized by the many people who watch these beloved films.

Works Cited

Bispo, Ashley. "Fairytale Dreams: Disney Princesses' Effect on Young Girls' Self-Images." *Dialogues Journal*. Rutgers School of Arts & Sciences English Dept., 17 April 2014. Web. 7 Nov. 2014.

Rosa, Jelani A. "9 Love Lessons From Disney Movies." *Seventeen.com*. Seventeen, 24 June 2014. Web. 10 Nov. 2014.

Saedi, Goal A. "Disney's 'Frozen' an Attempt to Modernize the Fairy Tale?" *Psychologytoday.com*. *Psychology Today*. Sussex Publishers, 26 Dec. 2013. Web. 10 Nov. 2014.

Whelan, Bridget. "Power to the Princess: Disney and the Creation of the 20th Century Princess Narrative." *Interdisciplinary Humanities* 29.1 (2012): 21–34. *Academic Search Premier*. Web. 10 Nov. 2014.

These movies enforce the idea that every story has a happy ending...

ALESSANDRA CARAVAGGIO

Instructor: Vana Derohanessian

UNREALISTIC RELATIONSHIPS IN DISNEY MOVIES

Disney movies, while cute and apparently innocent, often portray unrealistic examples of romantic relationships. Many Disney movies send implied messages to their audience. This is common in movies adored by the world such as *Enchanted*, *Sleeping Beauty*, *Cinderella*, and *Tangled*. [Though these movies may seem innocent, they really are influencing people of all ages into believing things that may not be true.] *Thesis*

In the majority of Disney movies, it is not unusual to see the two major characters playing the roles of Prince Charming and the Damsel in Distress. As the Prince or hero of the story is introduced, he appears to have very few flaws. Prince Charming usually looks handsome, with a charming personality, and many potential brides. On the other hand, the Damsel in Distress appears beautiful, with a great singing voice, and in need of someone to save her. For example, the hero in *Tangled* is Flynn Ryder, who rescues the troubled Rapunzel from her terrible stepmother who kept her "daughter" from the world. One day, Flynn Ryder shows up and gives Rapunzel the perfect opportunity to escape her life of being hidden from the world. Eventually, Rapunzel has the chance to become a princess again and live a much better life. This only happens because her hero saves her from a life that was miserable. In the end, her Prince Charming solves all of Rapunzel's problems.

Although having a Prince Charming is a very pleasant idea, it is unrealistic. There is no perfect man out there to save every girl from all her problems. There are many girls who have to save themselves from their own troubles. Girls typically imagine a perfect man. What they do not realize is that there is no perfect man with a charming personality and flawless looks. In Natalie Thomas's article, "Attention Ladies: Prince Charming Doesn't Exist," she states, "Ladies with their mile-long, superficial lists, the ones who dress themselves up and dumb themselves down for the VIP crowd, hoping for, perhaps getting the coveted man who will make their fairy tale dreams come true, where does that lead? For most, unlucky and unhappy in love." These ladies are looking for something that is nonexistent, and in the end, they wind up disappointed.

As we continue watching these movies, we will almost always see "love at first sight." As these characters interact with each other, they almost immediately fall in love. Usually this is followed by marriage and "happily ever after." In Disney's *Enchanted*, as soon as Prince Edward lays eyes on the young lady, Giselle, they fall in love and Prince Edward states: "We shall be married by morning!" Right before this wedding takes place, the two characters "in love" are separated. Prince Edward ends up risking his life to find a girl he hardly knows, so that he can marry her right away. Though Prince Edward does not marry Princess Giselle, he does end up marrying a different woman minutes after he meets her because he thinks she is beautiful and that he is in love. These Disney characters follow the idea that "love at first sight" is a real thing that can lead to marriage almost immediately.

Because people are seeing "love at first sight" in these movies, they begin to expect the same thing in real life as well. However, love is a process; it is not something that happens immediately. When a girl meets a guy, they do not fall in love right away and run off to get married. They usually take the time to get to know each other and eventually they may or may not fall in love and get married. You can't possibly be in love with a person you have just met. Love takes time to develop and grow. As Neely Steinberg writes, "It takes time to develop trust, vulnerability and real intimacy. It's not just about the good times and laughs. It's about loving someone despite their idiosyncrasies...it's also about feeling a sense of peace, comfort and emotional safety with someone. These things take time to develop." Steinberg explains what you have to go through to get to love in a relationship. She makes it clear that getting to know someone and learning to love him or her for who they are, helps your relationship develop into true love.

As you get to the end of almost every Disney movie, it usually concludes with the words "And they all lived happily ever after." These movies enforce the idea that every story has a happy ending with no conflict to tear anything apart. These movies teach that after overcoming an obstacle, everything will end up in happiness, where nothing goes wrong and everyone is content. At the end of *Cinderella*, she marries her Prince Charming and is saved from the life she once had; now she lives in a castle with no worries in her life. Again, this is seen in *Sleeping Beauty*, where she goes through the hardship of a deep sleep, and after being saved by her prince, they live happily ever after. The end goal of all these movies is to lead the audience to believe that, after going through troubles in life, you will have your "happily ever after" and everything will be okay.

At the end of the day, there are many couples who end up getting divorced after being married, because they are fighting a lot or are not as in love as they had thought. Couples begin to fight and argue over tons of things, big and small. Some stay in these relationships, attempting to endure the pain, while others break it off. This is not "happily ever after." Eric Barker writes in his article, "How to Live Happily Ever After According to Science," "Happily ever after ain't easy… About 50 percent of couples get divorced. Another 10–15 percent separate but do not file paperwork. And 7 percent are chronically unhappy." This shows how common it is for couples to live lives that are not like fairy tales.

Some people would argue that the movies are simply "cute" and "innocent." Some believe that movies are created for the sole purpose of entertaining viewers. They think that there is no ulterior motive in using cute phrases such as "love at first sight" or "happily ever after." Others are now trying to change this idea and tell us that "true love" is not only between a prince and his princess, but between sisters as well. In one of Disney's newer movies, *Frozen*, Disney portrays this new idea that a prince or hero is not needed for "true love." The new idea is that love within a family is enough to cure any hardship. Though this may be true to a degree, most Disney movies in the past claimed that for love to be truly successful, it must be between a prince and princess, and this is what young ladies and gentlemen are striving for in our world today.

As a result, we see that these Disney movies that are supposed to be harmless for children, end up affecting them. People of all ages believe what they are subtly being told. Children grow up believing that one day they will find their prince or princess and it will be love at first sight and end in "happily ever after." However, these messages are not true and Disney is portraying these romantic relationships as something they are not.

Works Cited

Barker, Eric. "How to Live Happily Ever After, According to Science." *The Week Magazine*, 6 May 2014. Web. 23 Nov. 2014.

Enchanted. Dir. Kevin Lima. Perf. Amy Adams, Patrick Dempsey, and James Marsden. Disney, 2007. DVD.

Steinberg, Neely. "Why You Shouldn't Believe in Love at First Sight." *The Huffington Post*. TheHuffingtonPost.com, 11 Sept. 2012. Web. 23 Nov. 2014.

Thomas, Natalie. "Attention Ladies: Prince Charming Doesn't Exist." *The Huffington Post*. TheHuffingtonPost.com, 19 July 2012. Web. 23 Nov. 2014.

> *As an elementary school student, the idea of being*
> *"gay" never came to my attention.*

Marc Ninapaytan

Instructor: Sharon Lim

The "Norm" Isn't So Norm

In some aspects, being gay or living a gay lifestyle is becoming more accepted, but the fight isn't over. I'm here to use my voice and claim my rights. As a homosexual male, I will keep projecting my voice until my rights are as equal as those of any straight person. Writing creatively and being exposed to various LGBTQA texts have engaged me to become more active and open about myself.

As an elementary-school student, the idea of being "gay" never came to my attention. What did come to my attention were things like nap time, recess, and of course, cooties. Although this may seem like an ordinary elementary-school experience, it wasn't. Many students mocked my voice. According to them, it was "too feminine." I couldn't understand this because I was a growing child. I wasn't hurt until another student started whipping me with his belt as if he had the right. I had to see this kid every day until I finished elementary school. I was young and so deeply traumatized that I could not speak up for myself.

Entering middle school was meant to give me a fresh start, but instead, my problems from elementary school rolled over to middle school. Being bumped around was child's play; instead, I was beaten in the restroom and had my backpack filled with urine and leftover lunch. Why didn't I say anything? I was frightened to death that something worse would happen to me. What was even more traumatizing about this experience was how my own cousins played a part in this situation. Being that they're my family, I should have received some sort of aid or protection, right? Wrong. I never understood why they chose to see me physically beaten every day, bumped around, or vocally harassed. My feminine voice, along with the way I walked, was criticized. The sad part was that I didn't even know who I was or why I had different sexual orientation labels thrown at me at such a young age. No one at this age should have a sexual orientation forced upon them; that's insanity. Thankfully, middle school ended and high school finally came around so that I could get to know new people. For the record, all of those horrible bullies from middle school ended up attending a different high school. Although they weren't there to bully me, the bullying continued until I finally spoke up for myself.

In my sophomore year, I was assigned a paper for English class called a "This I Believe" essay. We were given the assignment in order to feel comfortable with writing. The prompt was our free choice, so we were to write about anything we chose. During this time, I was going through family struggles: I was coming out to my own parents as gay. My father accepted me, but my mother never could. She was unable to understand my preferences. I understood that she needed time to process her thoughts. My "This I Believe" essay included my personal struggles with family, bullies, and myself. When I read this essay in front of the class, they were both shocked and mesmerized at my ability to speak on such a delicate situation. Throughout my reading, I stood strong until the very end when I cried, and my peers felt empathy for my situation. My peers were engaged by my essay and agreed that we should be who we are and speak our minds, rather than conform to what everyone else sees as "normal."

In high school, I was exposed to LGBT literature that related to the experiences I had to overcome. Reading these texts allowed me to see clearly that I wasn't the only one who had overcome such terror. I understood that my terrors were global. I became an advocate of change. Through the many LGBT readings, from freshman year to senior year, I came to the realization that I must take the steps in order to create the change I want to see. To many of my peers, I became the symbol of success and change. They read all my work and my teachers ended up showcasing my writing to every class and continue to showcase them to their English classes each year. This will help other students bloom into whoever they are.

There was no longer an issue or struggle with figuring out my sexuality. The next step was to speak up for myself in the event of bullying. The next time someone attempted to harass me, I spoke out and made sure to get the school involved. I raised awareness of the bullying that students faced. Many others supported me and made sure that the "No Bullying" policy was upheld. I ended up becoming president of the school's Tolerance Club, where we discussed many issues. We provided a safe environment for anyone who needed help. This club was inclusive and involved students of all cultures and backgrounds. My faculty advisor saw me as a peer model who would one day be very successful. As I became more involved with different clubs, I built a chain of friends who supported me and understood all my obstacles, as I did theirs. Now that I'm starting a fresh year at CSUN, I will continue to explore and build a pathway. I will not be overlooked. I will fight for the change that I want to see in the future.

> *...every couple deserves the right to marry and have access to the laws that bind and protect these unions, because love is love.*

LIZ HERWIG
Instructor: Mary Shannon

GAY MARRIAGE AND THE CONSTITUTION[1]

Same-sex marriage has recently been deliberated in our courts, and it has been protested for and against in the streets. People have different views on gay marriage and whether or not it should be legalized. Those who support same-sex marriage do so because they seek equality for same-sex couples and want those couples to have access to the same legal protections and rights that heterosexual couples are granted. People who do not support gay marriage usually feel this way because of strong religious backgrounds that teach them that homosexuality is wrong or unnatural. Despite the controversy, gay marriage has been legalized in several states and this is predicted to have a domino effect on the other states in time. Although some feel that same-sex marriage is not a "true" marriage because it is not between a man and a woman and cannot produce shared biological children, I believe same-sex marriage should be legalized in all states; I feel that every couple deserves the right to marry and have access to the laws that bind and protect these unions, because love is love. I also strongly believe that same-sex couples can be just as successful at parenting as heterosexual couples.

In theory, everyone is granted equal rights and protection under the Constitution. That being said, all couples, both heterosexual and homosexual, should have the right to get married. Marriage should not be just between a man and a woman. It should be made available for anyone who wants to commit his or her life to another person. Marriage is an institution that should exist separate from religion. That is why I agree with Kenji Yoshino when he talks about Judge Walker's ruling on same-sex marriage in California. He states that once Judge Walker removed the religious arguments behind Proposition 8's supporters, they could only "offer rationales so threadbare that they could not survive even the mildest form of constitutional scrutiny" (Yoshino). This means that when religious reasons are taken out of the argument about

---

1 *The Supreme Court ruling legalizing same-sex marriage nationwide was announced June 26, 2015, as* New Voices *was going to press. —Editors.*

the constitutionality of same-sex marriage, as it should be, there is very little to say against it.

Another reason I support the legalization of same-sex marriage is that homosexual couples deserve access to the same laws that protect heterosexual married couples. When a person is legally married, that person has the right to benefits earned by his or her spouse. This can include health benefits, life insurance, Social Security, and other forms of compensation due to injury or death of a spouse. Homosexual couples, on the other hand, often do not have these same protections—even if they are in recognized "domestic partnerships"—as Andrew Koppelman mentions in his article, "Judge Walker's Factual Findings." Some may argue that domestic partnerships are equivalent to traditional marriages, but without giving these same-sex couples the same legal rights and the title of "marriage," I feel this is another case of separate, but not equal.

Another issue I feel strongly about is ensuring that all married couples, including same-sex couples, should be allowed to raise or adopt children. Starting a family is a goal for many couples, and the sexual orientation of the parents should not exclude them from achieving that goal. As Yoshino states, "The claim that children raised by opposite-sex couples fare better than children raised by same-sex couples has been soundly refuted in the social science literature." This means that homosexual parents can raise children just as well as heterosexual parents. It should not matter if the couple is of the same sex because, if they can love and give support to a child, they have just as good a chance raising a child successfully as any other couple.

The opponents of same-sex marriage are very vocal in their arguments against it. Usually, their first argument is that same-sex marriage is not a "real" marriage because the example does not appear in the Bible, or because it is not traditional. They often use the argument that marriage has always been defined as between a man and a woman, so it would be wrong to change the law as it was written (Yoshino). These people may also argue that homosexuality itself is sinful, and therefore those who are gay should not be able to participate in the institution of marriage at all. People have these feelings about homosexuality and same-sex marriage either because it is what their parents or religion has taught them all their lives, or because they hold strong, conservative personal beliefs. The concept of the "domestic partnership" has been adopted by some states as a compromise between the proponents and opponents of same-sex marriage. This allows committed same-sex couples to access some of the same protections offered to married, heterosexual couples, but it falls short in some areas. It also withholds the title of "marriage" from same-sex couples, which satisfies some of those people who do not support gay marriage.

One of the biggest arguments against same-sex marriage, as voiced by Amy Wax in her article "Promoting the Ideal of Procreation," is the belief that because gay couples "cannot produce shared biological children" or are "sterile by their nature," then gay marriage will contribute to lowering the population rate or raise inferior children. Wax feels strongly that children who are raised apart from one or more of their biological parents are in a situation that is "tragic or regrettable, and…falling short of the ideal." She also feels these children will have problems forming a positive identity without the love and support of their natural parents. Whether adopted, born through surrogacy, or natural born, biological children of one of the same-sex partners, Wax argues that children raised by gay couples will be deprived of a "real" family and will not develop a true identity.

I believe that the majority of the claims made by the opposition to same-sex marriage are wrong. The argument that the only marriages that should be allowed are those that are "traditional," is weakened by the fact that our laws regarding "traditional" marriage have changed in our recent past to allow, for example, interracial marriage. People who say that because marriage has always been one way, it should stay that way, are too close-minded or not aware of how culture progresses and changes over time. Many feel that because same-sex marriage is not in the Bible, it is wrong. My argument against that is the Bible is a very old book, and much of what appears in the Bible is no longer considered acceptable in American society today, such as polygamy and slavery. Religious reasoning needs to be removed from the argument about the legality of same-sex marriage, and only the reason and logic present in the Constitution should inform lawmakers. The Constitution is a more relevant piece of writing, designed to promote equality for all Americans.

Every couple, same sex or not, deserves equal rights and should be allowed to have or adopt children. If a child is adopted by a gay couple, I do not feel that child will be deprived of a real family or not know who he or she really is, as Amy Wax and others argue. There are many examples of successful people who were raised by just one parent, or someone other than their natural parents. Very little is traditional today. Adoption—either by heterosexual or homosexual couples—is a good option for some kids because it can give them a better life than they might have had otherwise. As long as the parents are capable of loving and supporting the child, the sexual preference of the parents should not matter.

Everyone deserves equal rights. Access to marriage and all of the legal and social benefits it provides should be a priority for all citizens. The Constitution states that all have the right to "life, liberty, and the pursuit of happiness." Happiness, for most couples, consists of the right to love whomever they choose, commit to each other in marriage, and possibly start a family. For these reasons, I am in favor of legalizing same-sex marriage across the United States.

Works Cited

Koppelman, Andrew. "Judge Walker's Factual Findings." *The New York Times*, 4 Aug. 2010. Web. 18 Nov. 2014.

Wax, Amy. "Promoting the Ideal of Procreation." *The New York Times*, 4 Feb. 2014. Web. 17 Nov. 2014.

Yoshino, Kenji. "Too Soon To Declare Victory." *The New York Times*, 4 Aug. 2010. Web. 17 Nov. 2014.

ASSIGNMENTS

What Does the Writer Say?

1. Marc Ninapaytan, author of "The 'Norm' Isn't So Norm," describes the struggles he experienced as a gay teen in high school and how LGBT literature helped him see the world differently. Name a few contemporary books, television shows, or films that depict individuals who are different from "the norm." How are those characters portrayed?

2. Authors Liliana Valerio and Alessandra Caravaggio provide two particular viewpoints regarding the gendered messages in Disney films. If the two authors were having a conversation on this topic, on what points would they agree or disagree?

What Do You Say?

3. Alessandra Caravaggio provides a real-world perspective toward Disney movies normally admired by audiences. To what extent do you agree with the author? What specific examples can you provide to support your position?

4. What is meant by the term "gendered advertisements" in Susan Guthier's essay, "Toys and Gender in Advertising"? Think of a commercial or ad that you have seen recently. How is each gender portrayed in the text? Could it be considered "gendered advertising"?

Writing Exercises

5. For this exercise, write a 1–2 page analysis in which you respond to the following:

    In Liliana Valerio's essay, "Disney Princesses as Positive Role Models," the author sheds light on how contemporary Disney films actually provide young girls with positive female figures. Think of a recent film or television show intended for a young male or female audience. In what ways does that film or show provide its audience with positive, or negative, role models? Provide specific examples to support your claims.

6. For this exercise, write 1–2 pages analyzing and refuting the key points made in Liliana Valerio's essay, "Disney Princesses as Positive Role Models." (First, identify the key points that Valerio makes in her essay. Then, provide specific examples that could be used as evidence against Valerio's claims.)

7. For this exercise, analyze Liz Herwig's organizational choices in her argument essay, "Gay Marriage and the Constitution." To do this, first identify the main point in each of Herwig's body paragraphs. Then, discuss what paragraphs work well in Herwig's essay structure and what sections could be reorganized.

49

NOTES, RESPONSES, & IDEAS

Natalie Bedrosian & friend Nairi Nabi — Instagram photo for "Light the Night" event.

SECTION 4:
EXAMINING SOCIAL MEDIA

QUICK WRITE:

Based on your observations and experiences, what are the advantages and disadvantages of social media?

NOTES, RESPONSES, & IDEAS

> *My practical experience made me decide to focus on face-to-face relationships.*

Jeewon Lee
Instructor: Andzhela Keshishyan

Anti-Google, Not Anti-Social: An Exercise

STEP 1.

The result is zero.

STEP 2.

While searching for myself on Google, I am not surprised that my result is zero. I realized that I could keep my private information safe even if Google is telling people almost everything. I had previously gone through the process of blocking my information. While at a job workshop, three years ago, I heard a speaker in a presentation say, "Imagine your potential employer is searching you on Google." After hearing this, I realized that I did not want to show my private stories online. I wanted to minimize my information to strangers. I wanted to be assured that my personal information was successfully protected.

Through my whole childhood, whether I liked it or not, I had to change schools once every two years following my father's transfers. It meant that I moved more than ten times during my life, and I met a lot of new people almost biennially. While I wanted to keep in touch with my friends as much as possible, I found out it was not easy. Of course, when I was a naive elementary school student, I liked to keep in touch with my best friend. Since we felt we shared a lot of our lives and hobbies, we contacted each other for five years through letters. Unfortunately, however, after five years we no longer had any common conversation pieces; we felt we were living in different worlds. We grew away from each other. This story was repeated during my university life when I transferred to different universities in South Korea, and also when I became an exchange student in the United States. My practical experience made me decide to focus on face-to-face relationships.

ANTI-GOOGLE, NOT ANTI-SOCIAL: AN EXERCISE

If someone searches for me on Google and finds empty results, they might think I am anti-social. Yes, this reflects me, but just a part of me. This result does not indicate who I am because it is only one side of me. Can we figure out a person's personality in one moment in real life? No. The answer is the same on the Internet as it is in real life.

...donations to ALS charities soared within weeks of the challenge going viral.

Natalie Bedrosian

Instructor: Vana Derohanessian

LIGHT THE NIGHT[1]

The rise of social media throughout the past decade has, without a doubt, changed the lives of our generation. If you take a moment to think about social media, you might ponder whether this has brought about a positive or negative impact on our society. It is astonishing how much social media affects us in so many ways. It's tempting to turn to our phones for entertainment purposes when we are bored. Whether checking Instagram, Twitter, Facebook or surfing the web, the majority of the population is obsessed with their mobile devices because of social media. Can you blame our rapidly advanced high-tech society? We spread information faster than ever, along with raising awareness and money for good causes.

Instagram is a popular photo-sharing app, allowing millions of people to keep updated with each other, acting as a source of entertainment and advertising. Sharing photos on Instagram is a great way to raise awareness and share information. My friend and I joined and participated in "Light the Night," to make a difference in the lives of blood cancer patients and raise funds for the cause. By checking in at the event, posting our photo in front of the "Light the Night" poster, and captioning our photo with descriptive hash tags, we sent out a message to encourage people on Instagram to donate and attend the walk. This was an effective use of social media because many people immediately found out about the event and reached out to make a difference. If it weren't for social networking sites like Instagram, how would we spread information in such a quick and easy manner? The fact that individuals could instantly change the world for the better is definitely to our advantage. Think of all the ways we could benefit society by using social-networking sites to inform each other about important events, just by sharing. You know what they say: sharing is caring.

A recent trend on social-networking sites such as Facebook, Twitter, and Instagram, was the Ice Bucket Challenge, also referred to as the ALS Ice

---

1 See "Ebola and Social Media" in the "Confronting Illness" section for another viewpoint on this topic. —Editors.

Bucket Challenge. It became very popular on social media and many people started dumping buckets of ice over their heads, then recording and uploading video of it on the web to promote awareness of ALS (amyotrophic lateral sclerosis disease). Everyone who did the challenge had to nominate other people to do it. Not everybody wanted to dump ice on their heads, so whoever chose to forfeit made a donation.

The Ice Bucket Challenge was so popular that it was all over the news and showed many previews of peoples' uploads, ranging from celebrities to random individuals. Many people did not even know about the disease until the Ice Bucket Challenge went viral on social media. Public awareness and charitable donations to ALS charities soared within weeks of the challenge going viral. Pranoy Nair stated:

> Social networking has a great connect with the youth, be it any country. Whenever an interesting campaign reaches the block, it becomes an instant hit. I believe it is a very efficient way to spread awareness. It has already spread to an enormous number of people. Though some have been doing it for fun,...I am sure they come to know about the real cause. (qtd in Shetty)

Despite the many advantages that come with social media, many people, such as Stoney L. Brooks, who wrote "Social Media Usage: Examination of Influencers and Effects," do not think social media is all that advantageous. Brooks writes that many studies show that the greater the amount of time a user spends using social media, the greater the Social Media-Work Conflict they will experience. Many will have issues focusing on work when the time comes to pay attention (Brooks). Often, users will find themselves experiencing this conflict while at work or in the classroom.

The fact of the matter is that many people adhere to their phones and overuse social media, tending not to focus on hobbies such as sports, or going outside and appreciating nature. When thinking about what friends are updating or what is new on Twitter, working free of distraction seems like a struggle when it comes time to focus. The next time you find yourself on your phone for hours at a time, think about whether you are controlling social media, or whether it is controlling you. Make sure you are using social media wisely and not wasting your time.

Works Cited

Bedrosian, Natalie. "Instagram." *Instagram*. Natal_b, 28 July 2014. Web. 28 Oct. 2014.

Brooks, Stoney L. "Social Media Usage: Examination of Influencers and Effects." Order No. 3598043 Washington State University, 2013. *ProQuest*. Web. 26 Oct. 2014.

Geoff. "Who Started the Ice Bucket Challenge? ALS Association's Viral Fundraiser Has NY Roots." *Syracuse.com*. N.p., 18 Aug. 2014. Web. 28 Oct. 2014.

Shetty, Prashasti Satyanand. "The Chic Thing: Ice Bucket Challenge Creating a Buzz in City." *DNA : Daily News & Analysis*. Aug 27 2014. *ProQuest*. Web. 26 Oct. 2014.

> *SoulPancake, a growingly popular channel on YouTube,*
> *demonstrates these positive aspects of humankind…*

ALEXANDRA-JOYCE PORTE
Instructor: Vana Derohanessian

The Human Experience

Online social-media users have the authority to make this invisible virtual extension of social interaction anything they want it to be. YouTube, presenting a cross section of today's civilization, is a concoction of both pleasant and unpleasant content, streaming through a notional space–time continuum that directly reflects the nature of our society. Despite some shadowy darkness in its space, the positive take on YouTube is that it is a digital format of self expression, a connector between human beings, and a celebration of the milestones in life. SoulPancake, a growingly popular channel on YouTube, demonstrates these positive aspects of humankind in a whole new light. The SoulPancake community is all about tackling life's big questions and exploring what it truly means to be human in the context of spirituality, creativity, and philosophy. In other words, the community contributes to the goodness of society because it invests time in rich, opalescent spirits, and focuses all its energy on the golden profoundness of being human. More content like the videos that SoulPancake produces, which explore the true beauty of humankind, would encourage people to let their minds wander into new, uncomfortable, yet open-ended, in-depth conversations from a variety of perspectives. SoulPancake brings diverse people together to make a difference to the human experience.

The profoundness of being human is the ability to feel every possible thing traveling in our system: oxygen circulating throughout our lungs, a pulse throbbing at the tips of our fingers, a heart beating against our chest in the rhythm of a drum. Ultimately, the essence of feeling does not stop there. For, to be human, it is important to center ourselves and let our innermost feelings flow freely from our spirit in the colors of a double rainbow. Some might think that strong feelings should take the backseat because bottling up emotions in a jar seems far simpler than taking the risk and opening up the lid to examine complicated feelings. However, choosing the complicated over the simple is more exciting than sealing the jar, for "love and hate are beasts, and the one that grows is the one you feed" (Koyczan). If only two emotions exist, love and fear, then the universe must depend on humankind to choose the emotion that feeds hungry hearts and souls. For instance, SoulPancake uploaded a video on YouTube demonstrating that "everyone needs love in their lives, but sometimes it can be hard to find" ("Heart Attack"). In the beginning of the video, a mysterious white box on a busy boardwalk and a podium with a shiny red button both appear in the scene at Venice Beach. At the very beginning of the engaging broadcast, the upbeat strum of an electric guitar correlates with the scene of busy people walking by the props, not pausing for a moment. In the rush of people, only a few daring souls are brave enough to venture into the unknown and press the red button. The moment they press the button, an outburst of love shoots out from the box as voices sing with exuberant joy throughout the rest of the video. Perhaps the video is titled "Heart Attack" because you never know when you are going to be unexpectedly attacked by love.

After the button is pressed, a parade of people with heart-shaped faces, dressed in matching red-and-white outfits, dances right out of the box. They greet the surprised individuals while surrounding them with love, as expressions of wonder glow on their faces. Unleashing the warmth at the core of our spirit is an essential part of the human experience. It gives us hope that humanity can keep pressing forward on a grand scale, even when it is hard to find love. Because that is the critical thing: love is everywhere. The love attackers symbolize that love exists no matter who you are, where you are, or what time of day it is: "Need some love? Push here." The three words, "We Love You," written in white, are lit by a red, passionate, sunset glow. In the end, we all deserve love.

In due time, YouTube will be overflowing with content about "stuff that really matters," regarding all of life's biggest questions (SoulPancake). YouTube is making a difference in society because it is becoming more of a space for "storytellers determined to create media with meaning by focusing all of our energy on positivity" (Skoll). The YouTube community is inspiring acceptance and the celebration of life. According to Jeff Skoll, there are two gaps to be overcome in order to spark change: "One is the gap in opportunity—but perhaps the other, bigger gap is what we call the hope gap…And so chapter one really begins today, with all of us, because within each of us is the power to equal those opportunity gaps and to close the hope gaps." Applying his words to the relationship between social media and society, it is within human nature to save the world. Skoll explains that "our mission is to produce entertainment that creates and inspires social change. And we don't just want people to see our movies and say, 'That was fun,' and forget about it." Sharing and developing thought-provoking content can inspire change and explore the meaning of being human.

No matter how much negativity travels through the depths of social media, it is up to the people of the internet community to wise up. The bulk of social media shows that human beings are hungry for the human experience. YouTube works as a social mechanism that offers people a place to express themselves. SoulPancake is a catalyst for carrying the torch to unite all people by encouraging them to invest in making a difference and celebrating life and love as long as they live.

Works Cited

Koyczan, Shane. "Instructions For A Bad Day." *YouTube*. Shane Koyczan. 28 Feb. 2012. Web. 1 Dec. 2014.

Skoll, Jeff. Transcript of "My Journey into Movies That Matter." Jeff Skoll: "My Journey into Movies That Matter." N.p., Aug. 2007. Web. 28 Oct. 2014.

Soul Pancake. "Heart Attack." Online video clip. *YouTube*. 14 Feb. 2012. Web. 28 Oct. 2014.

ASSIGNMENTS

What Does the Writer Say?

1. For Alexandra-Joyce Porte, author of "The Human Experience," what does it mean to be human or to have a human experience? According to Porte, how does social media assist in the human experience?

2. Based on all three texts in this section, what are the positive and negative results of social-media use today? What rhetorical appeals are used by the authors to convince their readers of their arguments?

What Do You Say?

3. Natalie Bedrosian, author of "Light the Night," gives two specific examples of how social media allows individuals to make a positive contribution to society and to spread awareness for a good cause: Light the Night and the ALS Ice Bucket Challenge. Describe one or two similar social media "movements." In what other ways can people become involved in social causes online?

4. In "Anti-Google, Not Anti-Social," Jeewon Lee expresses her desire to focus more on face-to-face relationships and interaction. Think about the relationships in your life. In what ways do technology and social media make those relationships easier or more difficult?

Writing Exercises

5. In Jeewon Lee's essay, "Anti-Google, Not Anti-Social," the author begins by performing a Google search on herself and finds that "the result is zero." Perform a Google search on yourself, then answer the following questions:

   a. How easy or difficult was it to find yourself online?

   b. What web and image information stood out or surprised you? How much of the information did you know existed online?

   c. What might a potential employer think about these results if he/she Googled you after receiving your resume?

   d. Given what you were able to find online of yourself, to what extent do you agree or disagree with Lee's argument?

6. For this exercise, write a 1–2 page letter to an author in this section; choose the author whose argument regarding social media was most persuasive to you. In the letter, explain to the author why his or her argument was the most convincing, identify a point or two that you agree with and why, and pose some questions that you have after reading his or her text.

NOTES, RESPONSES, & IDEAS

CSUN's Earth Fair Cow — Photo by Marjie Seagoe

SECTION 5:
CONTEMPLATING FOOD

QUICK WRITE:

Write a detailed description of your favorite meal or experience with food.

NOTES, RESPONSES, & IDEAS

> *In Kuwait, the consumption of coffee is almost always a social experience...*

Abeer Almutairi

Instructor: Sandra Jackson

Drinking Coffee Alone in America

It is a strange thing for a girl from Kuwait to go into an American Starbucks store alone. I did this as part of my observation for a writing class. Of course, I had been to Starbucks many times. I like coffee as much as anyone else. I love Kuwaiti coffee, with its spicy smell and mix of beans with cardamom spice. I also like American coffee. Kuwaiti coffee is a constant. It does not change. It reminds me of the Kuwaiti desert that way. American coffee is different. It is like a canvas for a painting that can take different shapes. American coffee can be rich and sweet, or bitter and black. It can have a shot of espresso in it, or no caffeine at all. It can be big, small, or in the middle. It is as varied as America itself. Yet there are differences between American coffee and Kuwaiti coffee that have nothing to do with the taste, aroma, texture, or even the ways in which the coffees are brewed. In Kuwait, the consumption of coffee is almost always a social experience, but in America, coffee is too often consumed alone.

Penny De Los Santos makes the point in her TED talk video of how food can bring people together. She speaks of how she went to Lebanon to take photographs of a Ramadan meal. Ramadan is a Muslim religious holiday whose date varies from year to year. It is a time of penitence, reflection, and obedience to God. The holiday lasts for an entire month. During the day, those Muslims observing the holiday do not eat or drink. Food and drink are permitted only between sunset and sunrise. If Ramadan falls during the summer, when the days are long and nights are short, it can be a grueling holiday.

De Los Santos says that at the communal Ramadan meal that she photographed, what made the photographs special were the human subjects. The men participating were all from Iraq. They were refugees who had fled the war in their home country. Even though they were far from home, they had worked hard to put this festive meal together. The meal carried a symbolic meaning of friendship and faith. They all found special community in preparing and sharing. It gave them a special identity. There is a photograph of the men eating: the men sit on the floor, circled around the food, eating and talking. De Los Santos says that "food has the ability to peel away our differences and help us find a common language." Drinks like coffee have the ability to do the same thing.

I have been part of many Ramadan meals myself. They are called *eid* in Arabic. These meals are always communal. I cannot think of an *eid* that I ever ate alone. The food is wonderful. It tastes better because no one has eaten during the day. There is always delicious and aromatic Kuwaiti coffee served at the end of the meal. The coffee is like a warm candle, providing a glow for talk that goes into the night. This does not just happen at Ramadan. Most Kuwaiti meals are a reason to socialize and Kuwaiti meals are noisy from people talking and sharing. The preparation and serving of Kuwaiti coffee is a ritual that supports the community of the meal.

Contrast the image of a happy room of Kuwaitis lingering over their Kuwaiti coffee with my observations at the Starbucks in North Hollywood, California, on that Sunday afternoon in March. What I saw at Starbucks was many people drinking coffee in the same room, but little sense of community at the individual tables, even when people were there together. I saw many groups of friends that had coffee drinks. Some also had snacks. The Starbucks had plenty of tables for two, three, four, or even more people. Most tables were filled. However, few people talked as they drank their coffee. Most people were on their cell phones. The only table where people talked was filled with Asian students.

I tried to think of reasons why so many people would be texting or reading instead of chatting with their friends. It was not that the crowd was small, or tired from a long day of work or school. I was there on a weekend, and the place was full. There was every reason for people to have conversations. Starbucks is a friendly place. The tables are far enough away from each other to be comfortable, and there are even places to sit outside in the open air. There is nice music, colorful artwork, and even plenty of parking so that people do not need to depart in a hurry. Still, there was little conversation. It was almost as if the cell phones were controlling the people in the Starbucks, instead of the people controlling their cell phones.

Kuwait is different. One reason that the drinking of Kuwaiti coffee has such a social meaning is that Kuwaitis grow up with a special tradition called *dewaniya*. *Dewaniya* is an evening gathering in a Kuwaiti home where Kuwaiti coffee and sweets are served in order to help good conversation. Many Kuwaiti households have a special room for *dewaniya*, outside the main home. *Dewaniya* takes place nearly every night of the week. It is not an exaggeration to say that on any evening in Kuwait City, there are thousands of *dewaniyas* going on. It is a place for people to come and discuss social life, political developments, business, and family. It is also a place for people to introduce their friends to one another. Because of the *dewaniya* experience, where the tradition of conversation is tied to the ritual of making and drinking Kuwaiti coffee, people develop huge social networks.

For many years, *dewaniya* was limited to men. In recent years, though, women have begun to create their own *dewaniyas*. This is an approved part of Kuwaiti society. I myself have been the hostess for women's *dewaniyas* in my home in Kuwait City, and have attended dozens at the homes of others, where the aroma of Kuwaiti coffee always fills the air. Everyone prepares their coffee a bit differently. Some prefer a stronger mix, while others put emphasis on the cardamom. No matter how the coffee is prepared, though, no one would ever think of standing in a corner and drinking while sending an Instagram or checking their social-media status. Kuwaiti coffee plus *dewaniya* equals conversation and friendship.

Kuwait is not the only country where coffee and food are associated with social interaction. Many other countries in the Arab world do the same thing. Many non-Arab cultures, like Latino cultures, have a strong ritual tie of food to family and socializing. In her essay "Cherished Day," in *New Voices*, author Brenda Cardenas talks about a Latino family where the making of tamales is part of a holiday ritual that ends in a major family meal. The author of the short story seemed ambivalent about her family, but I think it is better to be ambivalent about people than filled with loneliness. I am not opposed to being alone sometimes. I have no problem with texting. But when I am drinking coffee with other people, whether it is American or Kuwaiti coffee, I want to talk with them. That is the way, as De Los Santos says, that food—and coffee!—can help us to find a common language. If Americans at Starbucks engaged with each other instead of disengaging, they might find the same joy that Kuwaitis enjoy when they share a pot of delicious Kuwaiti coffee.

Works Cited

Cardenas, Brenda. "Cherished Day." *New Voices*. Eds. Sandra Jackson & Amy Reynolds. Plymouth: Hayden-McNeil Publishing, 2015. Print.

De Los Santos, Penny. *Beyond Measure: TEDxAustin*. 28 Feb. 2012. Video. 21 Mar. 2015.

TAITO KUSAGAYA

Instructor: Sandra Jackson

FIRST AND FINAL DRAFTS

THE ROLE OF *NABE* AND ALCOHOL FOR JAPANESE PEOPLE (FIRST DRAFT)

The role of food would be helpful to bring people together even though they are culturally and characteristically different. Families in my country, Japan, often have a dinner together. Friends in Japan tend to hang out and have dinner and drink alcohol (in Japan the legal age for drinking is 20 years old). When food brings people together, it has three functions: help share information among people, and relieve mental stress. Especially Japanese *nabe*, which has many vegetables, meat, fishes and so on, in soup made by hot pot, is often used as one of the most popular tools to bring people together.

In Japan, I have experienced many situations related to food. We have dinner with family at home but as you grow up that scene becomes less. Many children in Japan start to join club activities like soccer, baseball, or basketball in junior high school. Moreover, some of them have a part-time job in high school. Thus, it tends to become more difficult to have dinner with family every night.

As each family member has less time for a dinner, they are likely to go to a restaurant instead of cooking by themselves. We often eat *nabe* because we have just one hot pot at the center of a table, and we are all round. This makes us feel united. This way, we can share dinner time with family. In addition, it will encourage us to get close to each other because we can share information. In my case, these days I do not have time to eat dinner with my family, so I have many stories that have not been told to them yet. When there is a chance to chat with them while eating dinner, we often talk about our stories about school, jobs, and so on. Talking about my life with my family makes us know each other's recent situations. I receive some advice about my life from my father or older sisters. For example, when we talked about my studying abroad, my older sister said, "You should use English when you meet foreigners even though you are now in Japan. You have to practice English." Sometimes, their ways of teaching me something are annoying, so I often avoid going to a restaurant with them. It is partly because, as I grow up, I want to make decisions by myself. In addition, their tones of voice sometime sound aggressive and they always criticize me, trying to find my weak points. I know they are very worried about me but it is annoying for me. My sense of family and food is opposite to the reading "Cherished Day," by Brenda Cardenas. She states, "On Christmas Eve, just like on any other holiday, it is very important for most of our family members to make it to the celebration. It is very rare when a family member can't make it for our Christmas Eve dinner" (92). Among her family, they almost always have Christmas dinner together. However, unlike her family, even on traditional Japanese holidays like *Oshogatsu*, New Year's Day, it is not rare for me to skip the dinner with my family.

I actually prefer to have a dinner with friends rather than with my family. My friends are not annoying like my sisters, because they kindly listen to me on any kind of topic and we can drink alcohol and talk about topics that we do not want to tell to our families. In fact, I often invite my friends to have dinner. Moreover, I also like to drink alcohol with dinner. Alcohol is helpful to relieve our stresses. Many Japanese people have serious problems related to work or school because there are many strict rules or customs that all people must follow. It is very easy for Japanese people to accumulate their stresses. However, once you drink alcohol, these complex social rules do not have to be followed: you can be frank with your bosses, or older people, who you must respect in many ways. Then, you can hear others' real thoughts which are hidden in their mind. For example, I have many friends who are usually quiet or calm. When they drink, their personalities dramatically change. They become noisy, laugh loudly, or even cry. One of my friends in the music club of my university in Japan often said, "I really love this club and the members! I am so happy in this club!" I feel that when they are drunk, I can directly touch their real emotions. This makes us get closer, although some of them tend to lose their memories of the time when they were drunk. Indeed, after drinking together, we often feel we get along with each other better. Many Japanese actually utilize drinking alcohol as a way of dissolving ice between coworkers. I believe that this tradition with alcohol is somehow unique to Japanese culture where it is difficult to open our real thoughts or ideas. Of course, it is not good to always drink alcohol: it will just cause alcoholism. Although many Japanese often drink after working, final exams, and so on, they usually have a clear distinction between fun time and serious work or studies. Overall, in Japan the role of food is to make better relationships between you and others.

Work Cited

Cardenas, Brenda. "Cherished Day." *New Voices*. Eds. Sandra Jackson & Amy Reynolds. Plymouth: Hayden-McNeil Publishing, 2015. Print.

Indeed, after drinking together, we would often feel we got along with each other better.

Taito Kusagaya

Instructor: Sandra Jackson

Nabe and Alcohol (Final Draft)

Nabe, the Japanese food of hot pot, can encourage family members to share their stories and get closer. Gathering around with the hot pot at the center of the table makes family members feel united and construct close relationships. This is because, as children grow up and become busy with their own studies or club activities, the chances to gather among family becomes less frequent. However, some children in Japan, like me, come to avoid having dinner with their family as they extend their range of lives from their family to outside activities. Instead of having dinner with my family, I would often hang out with friends and drink alcohol (in Japan, the legal age for drinking is 20 years old). Drinking alcohol in Japan plays surprising roles in relieving stress and hearing friends' real thoughts. Therefore, on the one hand, when people have problems outside of the family, they can share these stories with family while sharing *nabe*. On the other hand, people who do not like to have dinner with their family can have drinks with friends instead.

My family often eats *nabe* when we find a chance to get together for dinner. *Nabe* contains many vegetables, meat, fish, and so on, in a soup, and is often used to unite people. This way, my family shares dinner time and stories about our daily life. Usually, I did not have much time to eat dinner with my family, so I had many stories that I had not told them yet. When there was a chance to chat with them while eating dinner, we often talked about school, jobs, and so on. There, I received some advice on my life from my father or older sisters. For example, when I talked about my plan to study abroad, my older sister said, "You should use English when you meet foreigners, even though you are in Japan! You have to practice English!"

Sometimes, their way of teaching me was annoying, so I began to avoid having dinner with them because, as I grew up, I wanted to make decisions by myself. In addition, their tones of voice sometimes sounded aggressive and they often criticized me. I knew they were very worried about me studying abroad but it was just annoying for me. My sense of family and food is opposite from Brenda Cardenas, in her essay, "Cherished Day." Cardenas states, "On Christmas Eve, just like on any other holiday, it is very important for most of our family members to make it to the celebration. It is very rare when a family member can't make it for our Christmas Eve dinner" (92). Her family almost always has Christmas dinner together. However, unlike her family, even on traditional Japanese holidays like *Oshogatsu*, New Year's Day, it was not rare for me to skip dinner with my family.

I actually prefer to socialize with friends rather than family. My friends are not annoying, like my sisters, because they kindly listen to me on any topic and we can drink alcohol and talk about topics that we do not want to share with our families. In fact, I often invite my friends to have dinner and drink alcohol. Alcohol is helpful in relieving our stresses. Many Japanese people have serious problems related to work or school because there are many strict rules and customs that people are expected to follow in Japan. It is very easy for Japanese people to accumulate their stresses. However, once you drink alcohol, these complex social rules do not have to be followed. You can be frank with your bosses, or older people, who you usually must respect because of Japanese rules and manners.

Furthermore, people can hear others' real thoughts which are usually hidden in daily life. For example, I have many friends who are usually quiet or calm. But once they drink alcohol, their personalities dramatically change. They become noisy, laugh loudly, or even cry. I think this is because always hiding real thoughts or emotions causes serious stresses. One of my friends in the music club at my university in Japan often said, "I really love this club and the members! I am so happy I found this club!" I felt that when they were drunk, I could directly touch their real emotions. This made us get closer, although some of them tended to lose their memory of the time when they were drunk. Indeed, after drinking together, we would often feel we got along with each other better. Many Japanese students actually utilize drinking alcohol as a way of dissolving ice between club members or seminar groups. I believe that this kind of tradition with alcohol is somehow unique to Japanese culture, where it is difficult to reveal our real thoughts or ideas.

Of course, it is not good to always drink alcohol because it will cause alcoholism. However, although many Japanese often drink after hard work, such as final exams or performances at a school festival, they try to have a clear distinction between fun time, serious work, or studies. Overall, in Japan the role of alcohol is to make people relax and construct better relationships.

Japanese food, especially *nabe*, can help families share their stories about daily life and get closer. Or people can hang out with friends for dinner with alcohol to relieve stress and discover each other's real thoughts and emotions. In Japan, people construct different relationships, choosing to have dinner with family, or meet friends for dinner and alcohol.

Work Cited

Cardenas, Brenda. "Cherished Day." *New Voices*. Eds. Sandra Jackson & Amy Reynolds. Plymouth: Hayden-McNeil Publishing, 2015. Print.

> *I looked around the table and observed everyone's*
> *faces while they were eating; I saw joy.*

JIMENA ROSALES

Instructor: Sandra Jackson

LIFE IS JUST A BOWL OF *MENUDO*

Coming from a Mexican family, I grew up loving all traditional Mexican dishes. Every dish has its own unique taste, smell, and texture. Whether it is a family party or a holiday, food plays a major role in pretty much every Mexican celebration. It does not have to be a special dish; any dish is appreciated in my Mexican culture. It is not just about the process of making the food, it is about food bringing the family together. Food allows my family to interact with one another and share a bonding experience.

It was a Sunday morning, and as I woke up, birds were chirping and I could hear the noise of cars driving by. As I took off my blanket covers, I stretched my body and rubbed my eyes. I looked up to my dresser where my alarm clock was placed and read 9:00 a.m. After a busy week of school and babysitting, it felt so good to wake up after 7:00 in the morning. I slipped into my pink fluffy slippers and walked toward my television to play some pop music to start off my morning. As I headed to my closet to pick out an outfit, I noticed noises coming from the kitchen: I heard Spanish music, the sound of blending, knives chopping, and people chit-chatting and laughing. I was not expecting company so early in the morning.

As I finished getting ready, I walked out of my room and into the hallway. I peeked my head out of the hallway door to see what the noise was all about. I saw my parents, my aunts, uncles, and cousins in the living room. I stepped out to greet them. My face was filled with joy at seeing my family together and smelling delicious food. This meant we were either celebrating a special event or a family reunion. I walked over to the kitchen where my mom was cooking and asked her if a special event was going to be celebrated. She grinned, "*No mija, domas nos vamos ajuntar para comer menudo.*" (No sweetie, we are just getting together to eat *menudo*). When she said "*menudo,*" my mouth began watering and my stomach growled.

Menudo is not a dish we make often. Since it is a traditional Mexican dish, my family cooks it only on special occasions. *Menudo* is a type of beef soup with a spicy flavor. It takes a whole night to let the beef simmer, allowing it to get super soft. On the kitchen counter I saw cabbage, onions, garlic, and red chili peppers ready to be chopped into small square pieces. I looked through the kitchen window to the backyard and spotted my dad and uncles with packages of sodas, water bottles, and juice. They placed them in a refrigerator that we have in our garage. My dad then got the grill out to prepare hotdogs and hamburgers for the little kids.

As I sat down at the kitchen table, my mom said, "*Puedes ir a la marketa para agarrar platos y vasos?*" (Can you go to the market and get plates and cups?) My mom always sends me out to the market to get last minute things. I jumped into my car and rushed to buy what my mom had told me to get. Surprisingly, it took me only about 20 minutes to get to the market and back home. As I returned, I saw the men placing tables and folding chairs on the green grass in the backyard. I got the plates from my car and placed them on one of the outside tables. Then I helped bring out the desserts while everyone else helped bring out the utensils, salsas, and other food.

As usual, the little kids had the option of getting hot dogs or hamburgers, since they did not like *menudo*. The kids thought the meat looked different and was disgusting. While the kids were enjoying their meals, my uncles were seated and my aunts served them each a bowl of *menudo*. Then it was time for my aunts to serve themselves. Before I began eating, I brought out some *tostadas* to dip into the soup. One way of using the *tostadas*, even though it gets messy, is to scoop up the meat. I finally took my first scoop of *menudo*; nothing had changed. It was still as squishy as it could be, and the spiciness brought joy to my taste buds. I looked around the table and observed everyone's faces while they were eating; I saw joy. We laughed, and talked, and danced.

In her article, Hope Gillette explains the importance of food and family connection: "The missing piece of a puzzle when it comes to reaching Latinos about food choices is the family connection." These are the kinds of moments I enjoy the most with my family. We do not realize how food brings us together to interact with each other and cherish our culture. In a TED Talk video, photographer Penny De Los Santos said, "Food is the most honest and simple expression of who we are." She explains how food, the simplest thing, shows others where we come from and how our food brings people together. I strongly believe that food has an important emotional value in my Hispanic family; we eat when we are celebrating, sad, mad, excited, or nervous.

Works Cited

De Los Santos, Penny. *Beyond Measure: TEDxAustin.* 28 Feb. 2012. Video. 21 Mar. 2015.

Gillette, Hope. "Latino Food Purchases Most Influenced by Family, Emotional Values." *Voxxi.* Interactive One Publications, 05 Aug, 2013. Web. 21 Mar, 2015.

> *...short-term diets are not the way to lose and keep the weight off.*

Kayla Nehorayan

Instructor: Jaclyn Hymes

Fad Diets Are the Wrong Choice

Many people, including celebrities, want a diet that shows results quickly, but the problem with most fad diets is that they are not diets for long-term success. Fad diets usually promise huge results in a short time. Many experts have written about the amazing results of fad diets like Jenny Craig, Weight Watchers, and others, but not everyone hears about the diets where people change how they live. Predictably, nutritionists will never recommend a fad diet, unless you are only looking for short-term effects. There have been many debates about whether fad diets work, or if changing how you eat is really the only way to lose weight. Although many celebrities use fad diets, these diets have only a short-term effect, while changing your lifestyle and how you eat have long-term effects and allow people to keep the weight off.

Louise Davie, a writer for *Good Housekeeping*, wrote about how there have been many spokeswomen for Jenny Craig; Valerie Bertinelli is one of them. Davie stated that Bertinelli struggled with her weight for decades, but when she joined Jenny Craig, she was able to lose over twenty pounds. Bertinelli started at a size 12 and "just a few months later, Valerie reached her goal: an incredible 40 pounds lost" (Davie). Davie seems to prove that the Jenny Craig diet does result in success and that it is an easy way to eat and enjoy yourself while you lose the weight, until you reach your goal. Bertinelli has also appeared on Rachel Ray, speaking about her success while on the Jenny Craig diet. Many other spokeswomen have also lost weight on this diet and others. However, there are a few things not shown in this article that prove fad diets are not the route to take.

Lindy West proves Louise Davie wrong in a quick second. She describes these spokeswomen gaining the weight back and having to start Jenny Craig all over again in order to lose the weight they put on. Kirstie Alley lost 75 pounds with Jenny Craig in 2004, but after leaving in 2007, gained 30 pounds. She even said to *People* that she was good for a bit and then the weight just crept back. Alley ended up launching her own fad diet called Organic Liaison Weight-Loss System and lost 100 pounds (with the help of also competing on

Dancing with the Stars). After stopping all that, Alley's weight crept back up. When Alley started Jenny Craig again, she used the excuse that she loved having a coach and that she did not think anyone could "make it for the long haul" without one. West stated:

> I'm not sure if this makes her the worst spokesperson ever ('Hey! This program doesn't actually change your body and habits in any significant long-term way at all—just look at me!!') or the *best spokesperson ever* ('Hey! The only way you'll ever achieve long-term weight loss is to STAY DEPENDENT ON THE JENNY CRAIG CORPORATION AND GIVE THEM ALL OF YOUR MONEY FOREVER').

This is not the first time Alley has gained weight after leaving Jenny Craig. She is one of the best examples of a yo-yo dieter, someone who starts a diet, loses weight, goes off the diet, gains the weight back, and starts the diet all over again. There have also been various articles and pictures of Valerie Bertinelli, who seems to have gained most of the weight back as well.

Another example of why fad diets are not the best is in the article "Diet Fads Seldom Yield Results," by Karen Rudolph Durrie, who claims that the majority of fad diets and weight-loss programs that give the user quick results are hard to maintain. Lindy Kennedy, a registered dietitian and a certified personal trainer, agrees that short-term diets are not the way to lose and keep the weight off. Erin Pelletier is someone who spent thousands of dollars on a packaged-food program. She told Durrie that she felt great at first and lost a lot of weight in a few months, but as time went on, it got more difficult. After losing 42 pounds while on the program, she stopped using it and gained 46 pounds back. She then decided to "swear off the quick fix and go for slow and steady to win the race" (Durrie).

To have a suitable diet that will help you lose weight and keep it off, you must start with complex carbohydrates, proteins, and colorful fruits and vegetables that contain a bunch of antioxidants. Kennedy discusses how people focus on counting carbohydrates and fat, when they should really be counting the calories. There are three ways your body can go when eating calories: if you eat more than you burn, you gain weight; if you eat the same amount you burn, you stay the same; but if you eat less than you burn, then you will lose weight. It is as simple as that. The best way to lose weight and keep it off is just not fast enough for most people in this society. Durrie provides evidence throughout her article for why fad diets do not stick, while long-term diets do. She confidently states that those who have sensible and healthy eating habits, who exercise regularly and view dieting as a lifestyle rather than a punishment, will achieve their goals and find success.

I have had personal experience with trying to lose weight. My mother would start me on all these diets, from Weight Watchers to the 7-Day Diet to Lindora and many more. None of them ever worked for me. I either gave up because they were too difficult to follow, or I got physically sick from what I was supposed to be eating on these diets. I remember the 7-Day Diet was probably the toughest. I had to eat nothing but protein for three whole days. That may not seem difficult, but without fruits and vegetables, I constantly got headaches and did not have the energy to get out of bed. I did not make it past the second day and did not see any progress in losing weight. After struggling for years trying to lose weight, I was 180 pounds at the age of 16. I was depressed and shy because I did not have any confidence. That is when my father hired a nutritionist to help me. The nutritionist told me it was not going to be easy and fast like most diets, but it would be worth it in the end. During the first week, I was allowed to have a piece of bread in the morning with some protein, two protein snacks a day, and protein with vegetables and fruit for lunch and dinner. I would also need to drink about four bottles of water a day. I ended up losing five pounds in the first week, but then it became more difficult because, as time passed, I did not lose as much weight. My nutritionist explained to me that I just needed to push myself to get to my goal weight, and finally I did. Two-and-a-half years later, l reached my goal of losing 48 pounds and have kept it off since then because I learned how to eat and change my lifestyle for good. Now I can go out and enjoy myself but I know how to maintain my weight so that I do not gain it all back.

Fad diets are not as special as they may seem. Whenever people lose their weight and have reached their goals, studies have shown that they usually gain it back, mainly due to the fact that they rely on the diet telling them how to eat. Once they get off the diet, they are on their own and usually do not know how to eat in the real world and do not understand portion control. Changing one's lifestyle, and learning how to eat on a daily basis, will help people to keep the weight off and enjoy life more. Just as Erin Pelletier said, slow and steady will win the race.

Works Cited

Davie, Louise. "Valerie Bertinelli's Weight-Loss Victory." *Good Housekeeping*, 1 Feb. 2008. Web. 12 Nov. 2014.

Durrie, Karen Rudolph. "Diet Fads Seldom Yield Results." *Calgary Herald*, (2006) N 15. 9 Nov. 2006. *LexisNexis Academic*. Web. 3 Nov. 2014.

West, Lindy. "Kirstie Alley Gained A Bunch of Weight and is Back with Jenny Craig." *Jezebel*, 7 April 2014. Web. 12 Nov. 2014.

Assignments

What Does the Writer Say?

1. In "*Nabe* and Alcohol," what does writer Taito Kusagaya identify as the parallel between *nabe* and alcohol?

2. Abeer Almutari uses coffee as a kind of metaphor for social behavior in her essay, "Drinking Coffee Alone in America." How does she use this metaphor to remark on two different cultures?

What Do You Say?

3. Taito Kusagaya claims in "*Nabe* and Alcohol" that *nabe* plays a unique role in Japanese culture. Do you have a dish that plays a similar role in your family or your culture? Explain.

4. Describe the organizational pattern in "Life is Just A Bowl of *Menudo*." Do you think that the structure is justified by the subject matter of the piece? Explain.

Writing Exercises

5. For this exercise, write a 1–2 page reflection using "*Nabe* and Alcohol," by Taito Kusagaya, as a model. Focus on the following:

   Kusagaya explores the way that friends begin to play a larger role in his life at the expense of time with his family. Have you experienced a similar trade-off in your own life? Explain.

6. For this exercise, read "Fad Diets Are the Wrong Choice," by Kayla Nehorayan, and write a 1–2 page argument in which you address the following:

   Nehorayan claims that fad diets are not long-term solutions to weight issues because they do not permanently alter our relationship with food. What other complicating factors affect Americans' relationship to food? Are economics a factor? Convenience? Is it about health?

"Fields of Wheat" by Ani Muradyan

SECTION 6:
CONFRONTING ILLNESS

QUICK WRITE:

Describe your thoughts and emotions as you examine the above photograph. What, in your opinion, is the link between the photograph and the topic of illness?

Notes, Responses, & Ideas

> *I come from a perfectly imperfect childhood.*

Lorena Robertson

Instructor: Stephanie Lim

Grandpa's Legacy

Growing up in a household where my father was an alcoholic, I did not have an ideal childhood. Fighting between my parents became the norm. They constantly threw stuff at one another, my mother dumped beer down the drain, and of course, both slammed the door before leaving the house. The anxiety of whether or not we would stay together as a family always caused a hopeless feeling among my four siblings and me. What hurt me most was not being able to have a father–daughter relationship.

I did not like being home alone with my father; I feared him because of the violence I witnessed between him and my mother. I was my mommy's little girl and didn't like seeing her stress about my father when he left the house. As a teacher, my mother often had to stay late at school for parent conferences or meetings. I preferred to stay at my grandparents' house until she could pick me up, because I feared my father.

My grandparents' house was my safety blanket. There I had my Superman, my grandpa, the man I looked up to and who gave me the loving care my father would not show me. Every morning before my mom went to work, she would drop me off at my grandparents' house. My grandma would make me my favorite breakfast with lots of love, making not just any oatmeal, but one where I could taste all the love put into it: creamy, buttery, and rich. I would sit at the table with my loving grandpa and constantly make jokes with him. Anyone who walked into the house could feel the love we shared. After being fed, I would sit and watch TV on my grandpa's lap. No one really understood why I was so attached to him, why we had such a strong bond. I knew why: the absence of my father's love was more than filled by the affection my grandfather showed me, and it is something that I will never forget.

Even though my grandfather was already retired by the time I was born, he was still very active. For example, he would do work around the house for my grandma, take my cousin to school, take me to school, pick me up, and pick up my cousin. My grandpa and I had a routine every morning: we would enjoy a delicious breakfast, take my older cousin to school, go to the doughnut shop on the corner of Osborne and Arleta where he'd get me doughnut holes, and of course, as usual, my *abuelito* would buy lottery tickets. We would then go back, get me ready, and drop me off at my preschool. I always made my grandpa leave early because I wanted to be at the front of the line. My grandfather never failed to take me to school early, or to be on time to pick me up and ask, "How was school, *Lorenita la mas Bonita*?" I always replied with a smile on my face, "It went good, Grandpa." He was my hero. When I was with him, all the problems at home were a blur.

On January 11, 2001, my life changed. We were at my house and my grandparents were babysitting my cousin Doe-Doe and me. My dad was in the hospital at the time for knee surgery, so the Christmas lights were still up around my house; my grandpa decided he was going to take them down. One small activity changed my family's life. While on the roof, my hero suffered from a massive heart attack, and rolled off the roof. My grandma, my cousin, and I were inside when we heard a "thump." We quickly jumped up and ran outside, where we found my hero hopeless on the ground, unable to move. My cousin and I yelled, "*Abuelito*, wake up wake up!" My grandma sent me to tell the neighbor to dial 9-1-1. As I ran across the street to tell the neighbor, my grandma said her goodbyes to my grandfather. Seeing him put into the ambulance and sent off, I realized I should value all the time I have with my loved ones. January 11th was the last day I got to spend with my grandpa.

We gathered to see him lie peacefully in his casket. I did not want to leave his side. I was only four, and had lost someone I saw as a hero and a father, my Superman. I watched my mom break down, unable to deal with her significant loss. She soon began to use anger as her grief. This monster that had knocked on our door that dreadful day tore my family even more apart. My mom could not deal with my father's problem like she could before. She would explode like dynamite, with no warning. Picture frames would break in my home. My safety blanket was now in heaven, causing me to fear both my parents, because of the ammo they had stored up. The picture-perfect family in the family portrait in the living room was now broken, with sharp glass pieces sticking out.

Days became gray and nights grew long. No one smiled around my house. My house became haunted and no relative wanted to visit the location of my grandpa's death. Night after night, hearing my mother cry and yell at my father because she couldn't stand his drinking, I curled in a ball in the corner of a room with all my siblings, crying and praying that one day our lives would be normal and happy. My mom couldn't stand the thought that her father had just passed away, and that the next man who held her heart was slowly throwing his life away with every bottle he chugged. For four years, we lived in a world with no pigment, until we were struck by lightning one more time.

In December 2004, I was eight years old when my father was rushed to the hospital due to his excessive drinking and uncomfortable stomach pain. The night my father went to the hospital, I cried myself to sleep. I was not close to my father, but I realized I still loved him. I remember my siblings and I stayed home and my mom went to the hospital. At home, we gathered in one room, praying that my father would overcome this obstacle and come home to us. That night, my mother called the house letting us know not to stay up, because my father had been rushed into surgery; his drinking had caused severe organ damage. The doctors informed my mom that my father was lucky she had brought him in that day or he wouldn't have survived. The next day, he was rushed into surgery again due to the complicated disruptions he had caused to his organs.

Two days before Christmas and still my father had not been released. That night, we got news that my dad was going to be put under again and we were not sure if he was going to survive this surgery. My house turned silent. No one talked and all we did was cry together and pray for my father to come home, and stop drinking. God heard us and let my father live.

Weeks went by and every day after school we went to the hospital, sat with my dad, talked about our day, and did homework. He kept apologizing for the stress on the family, but there was no need for apologies. Everyone makes mistakes; all I wanted was for him to stop drinking completely. Slowly, I started connecting with my dad.

He recovered and was let out of the hospital. My father decided his drinking days were over and it was time to be a better dad. I grew close to my father to replace the hole in my heart where I had lost my grandpa. Every day I would come home excited after school because I got to play nurse with my father when his wound and his colostomy bag needed cleaning. I looked into the future and saw that if my dad could move forward from his dark days, then everyone else could.

Now, at seventeen years old and attending Cal State Northridge, I still hurt over the loss of my grandpa. That is something I will never forget. However, my childhood, with my father's dark days, I do tend to block out because my daddy is over those issues and is now the strongest man I know. He was able to completely stop his alcohol abuse, not only for himself, but to stay healthy to raise us. The bond my family now shares is stronger than ever. I have gone through many obstacles that have taught me to keep my head held high even through a storm. When people think I have a perfect life, I just smile because I know the truth. I come from a perfectly imperfect childhood.

Pegah Poordehghan

Instructor: Holly Batty

Euthanasia: Annotated Bibliography

Bevacqua, Frank, and Sharon E. Robinson Kurpius. "Counseling Students' Personal Values and Attitudes toward Euthanasia." *Journal of Mental Health Counseling.* Apr. 2013: 172+. *Health Reference Center Academic.* Web. 4 Nov. 2014.

The article focuses on different religions and their beliefs on assisted suicide and euthanasia. The article also focuses on how euthanasia is different according to the person's age, demonstrating how age is a very important factor in euthanasia. It also mentions how more people are supportive of euthanasia than they were years ago. Throughout the article, there are multiple citations from other sources to help the writers prove their point. The authors have more general and informative views towards the issue rather than having a biased opinion. It is objective, giving facts from both sides of the situation.

My topic is on euthanasia, so therefore, I will use this source to demonstrate how more people are open to euthanasia than they were multiple years ago, and also how the views of people have changed. This article was very useful in the sense that it gave the outlook of different people, and that can help me make my argument and prove my point.

Diaconescu, Amelia Mihaela. "Euthanasia." *Contemporary Readings in Law and Social Justice* 4.2 (2012): 474+. *Opposing Viewpoints in Context.* Web. 4 Nov. 2014.

This article describes euthanasia and how this controversial topic has been around for so long. The article talks about the different types of euthanasia and what they all mean. Also, it describes something similar to the procedure of euthanasia, called orthonasia. It explains how ethical and religious views play an important role in euthanasia. This source was listed under law and social justice and explains how the author sees the issue socially. This article uses other sources to support its claim. The text is biased in the sense that it agrees that euthanasia should be legal.

I agree with the article because I also argue that euthanasia should be legal. The source is helpful to my research by explaining how euthanasia should be legal and why humans should be able to make this decision. The opposing view will also help my readers understand my essay better and strengthen my argument.

Fenigsen, Richard. "Other People's Lives: Reflections on Medicine, Ethics, and Euthanasia." *Issues in Law & Medicine*, Summer 2010: 33+. *Health Reference Center Academic*. Web. 5 Nov. 2014.

This article gives an overview of medicine and euthanasia. The article goes into how nurses and hospitals treat their dying patients poorly. The article reveals how so many patients are refused treatment. It explores the idea of quality of life and how that has a part in euthanasia. Similar to the other articles, this one also uses other sources to prove its point. This article is biased in the sense that it is trying to argue that euthanasia should be legal, especially since hospitals are terrible and do not treat patients.

I also agree with this source because I believe that people should have the opportunity to make the choice whether they want to live and suffer, or to die. I will use this source to demonstrate how their arguments are similar to mine. This article can also be useful because it describes what patients have to go through in order to seek medical attention, and even then, they are not properly treated. The source can help me demonstrate the horrible hospital conditions that can lead to more people wanting euthanasia.

> *...social media has made Ebola the laughing stock of our generation.*

ELIZABETH ALTOUNIAN

Instructor: Vana Derohanessian

EBOLA AND SOCIAL MEDIA[1]

Thesis

Since the discovery of Ebola-infected people in America, many popular social networking sites, such as Twitter, have been mocking the actual severity of this illness without taking into consideration that these outbursts may lead to criminal charges or even exposure to this deadly virus. When it comes to Ebola, the younger generation believes that making jokes about it is acceptable. In other words, social media has made Ebola the laughing stock of our generation. The main reason people ridicule and mock a disease new to the American public is because of the lack of information provided to the public about this deadly illness. Therefore, our ignorance drives our judgment. The symptoms of this disease are so severe, they can lead to death; Ebola has put many people in quarantine and has killed many who have been exposed to the disease.

supporting the thesis statement

An example that demonstrates someone taking Ebola too lightly is a tweet that states, "If I get Ebola I know who I'm sneezing on first" (@Girlfessions). When the person tweeting states, "If I get Ebola," it implies that the person running this account is not thinking about what this disease will do to her, but thinking about what it can do to people she doesn't approve of. Threatening to spread the Ebola virus reveals the blatant ignorance of those in our society who are quick to stoop to ridiculous insults just to crack a joke. Another example is the post on Twitter using the very famous film, *Mean Girls*, as a joke implying that the main character Lindsey Lohan plays is the person who actually brought Ebola to the U.S. A picture posted of Lindsey Lohan's character is captioned, "We all know who really brought Ebola from Africa and into the USA…" This implies her character was the one who brought the disease because the character is from Africa (@TedOfficialPage). Using *Mean Girls* as the source of this joke appeals to a much broader audience because everyone, regardless if they have seen the movie or not, is familiar with this pop-culture reference. The more popular the film, the quicker these jokes (or memes) spread. The more common a joke becomes, the more socially acceptable it becomes to make fun of a deadly disease.

examples on jokes towards ebola on social media (twitter)

---

1 See "Light the Night" in "Examining Social Media" for another viewpoint on this topic. —Editors.

Younger generations who grew up on social-media sites might not understand the severity of their actions regarding the constant ridiculing of Ebola. There have been a few cases of criminal threat charges brought against people who thought it would be a good idea to joke about having the Ebola disease. NBC News reported on October 14th, 2014, that a passenger on a metro bus in the Lincoln Heights area claimed he had Ebola and authorities opened a criminal threat investigation against him. Apparently, "a man in a surgical mask told a bus driver, 'You better not mess with me because I have Ebola,' before getting off the bus" (NBC). What if the many off-color jokes about this disease inspired this particular man to take the joke even further? This man's outburst spurred authorities to open an investigation into the matter, because he made a joke he thought was socially accepted. This joke caused the whole bus to be put under lockdown until they were sure no one was infected. A similar incident occurred on an airline involving a man who made a joke about having Ebola before he was escorted off the plane: "Four officials in blue plastic hazmat suits boarded U.S. Airways Flight 845 to retrieve him after it landed in Punta Cana in the Dominican Republic" (KTLA 5). This man caused a panic because the disease was originally carried over by a man from Africa visiting his family in Texas. The jokes were probably meant to be harmless but because of the dangers of this particular disease, serious actions were taken against the people who made the jokes.

Humor is a way for people to communicate their fears to each other but there comes a point where these jokes can be abused. There are those people who claim that citizens have freedom of speech. Freedom of speech does give people the right to say what they wish: "Freedom of Speech, Right, as stated in the 1st and 14th Amendments to the Constitution of the United States, to express information, ideas, and opinions free of government restrictions based on content" (Britannica). People will argue that they can say what they wish without any consequences, just as people do on social media websites like Twitter. However, the hypothetical "fine print" of the amendment explains that it is limited to content. People have the wrong understanding of the amendment.

Social media can alter the way people view certain things in society but should not change the way we act in public. The Ebola jokes being made on Twitter and in public have completely different consequences. Society does have the right to freedom of speech, yes, but it all depends on how one puts it to use. With a disease so deadly, the government has the public's safety in mind. This is why such severe actions are being taken to make sure Ebola does not spread and infect more people than it already has.

[handwritten margin note: more examples / n people mocking / Ebola & threatning / any people / ...ding to / ...quences by / ...v't.]

Works Cited

"Freedom of Speech." *Encyclopedia Britannica*. CSUN Oviatt Library, 9 Oct. 2013. Web. 28 Oct. 2014.

Girlfessions (Girlfessions). "if I get Ebola I know who I'm sneezing on first." Re-Tweet. N.d.

Kandel, Jason, and Gadi Schwartz. "Ebola Scare Prompts Criminal Threat Investigation." *NBC Southern California*. N.p., 14 Oct. 2014. Web. 28 Oct. 2014.

Knight, Nerissa, and CNN WIRE. "Man Escorted Off Plane by Men in Hazmat Suits After Ebola Scare on US Airways Flight." *KTLA* 5. N.p., 9 Oct. 2014. Web. 28 Oct. 2014.

Ted. (TedOfficialPage). "we all know who really brought Ebola from Africa and into the USA…" 04 October 2014, 2:00 p.m. Tweet.

1 - Thesis

2 - A. what is said about Ebola on social media
    1. sneezing
    2. mean girls

3 - B. consequences by government
    1. bus
    2. airline

4 - C. freedom of speech - opposition
    1. limit
    2. actions

5 - Conclusion

ASSIGNMENTS

What Does the Writer Say?

1. In her essay, "Grandpa's Legacy," Lorena Robertson discusses her "perfectly imperfect childhood" through the lens of her father's disease. What was that disease and how did it shape her both as a child and as the woman that she is now?

2. The essay, "Ebola and Social Media," by Elizabeth Altounian, cites several sources from social media. Why did Altounian choose these non-academic sources? What other sources could she have used?

What Do You Say?

3. In Lorena Robertson's essay, "Grandpa's Legacy," the author describes her grandparents' house as a "safety blanket" and her grandfather as her "hero" and "superman." How do these analogies affect your reading of the story? Why do you think the author chose to use these particular terms, and what effect does it have on you as a reader?

4. Elizabeth Altounian examines both Ebola and social media in her essay, "Ebola and Social Media." How does she effectively balance these two disparate topics and make them relate to one another?

Writing Exercises

5. In "Ebola and Social Media," Elizabeth Altounian talks about the way in which social media can shape an issue like Ebola on a national scale. In what ways have recent social media trends shaped other health concerns? Respond to this question in 1-2 pages.

6. For this exercise, create an annotated bibliography for this section (Section 6) of *New Voices*.

   The annotated bibliography is a useful tool for keeping track of your sources and organizing your thoughts. Use Pegah Poordehghan's annotated bibliography as a model and create an entry for each of the texts in this section. Summarize each text in this section, then note the information you find most interesting and consider how you would use each of these texts in your own writing.

NOTES, RESPONSES, & IDEAS

SECTION 7:
TELLING DOG TALES

QUICK WRITE:

Do you consider yourself a dog person, a cat person, or neither?
Explain.

Notes, Responses, & Ideas

Matthew's face lit up and he yelled, "A puppy! What kind of dog is it, Josh?"

JOSHUA CORONA
Instructor: Holly Batty

DOG DAYS

Click. The nozzle at the gas pump set into place after I filled up my tank. As I opened the door to my '98 Corolla, I was carefree, with a beautiful Saturday evening ahead of me. I started the ignition and stepped on the accelerator. I pulled out of the gas station and looked both ways before I exited right. Claremont streets were always empty on the weekends; most families were out watching their youth play soccer or baseball. As I admired the clear roads, I softly pulled up to the cross streets of Claremont Blvd. and Monte Vista Avenue. A red light stopped me in my tracks, forcing me to scan the area to the left and right of my car. I peered toward my left and saw a box with a word in black bold letters that read, "**FREE.**"

This box of mystery was in front of an office building, not a residential area. A flash of green brought me back from my pondering. I pulled up next to the box and slowed to a stop. I exited my car, while the engine ran. I hovered over the box and inside was the cutest little brown puppy I had ever seen. It was as big as both my fists put together, the paws no bigger than my thumb print, with eyes that could stare into your soul and relieve you of any darkness within. A note hung on the inside of the box. With one hand, I stroked the dog's head, which was soft, with hair as short as a newborn baby's. With the other hand I reached for the note: "Free puppy! If still here by 4:30 pm I'll be forced to put it down." The handwriting was scratchy and I could tell it had been written quickly. I glanced at my watch: 4: 15 pm. Without hesitation, I put the furry critter in my car and drove off.

The puppy whimpered, so I comforted him with a loving hand. He seemed so fragile; I felt that if I were to pet him too hard, his bones would shatter. While driving, I was careful with every maneuver I made. I eyed my speed, surroundings, and the pup, all at the same time. When I made my last turn, I realized I had completely forgotten my parents. They had no idea that I was about to bring another life into our home.

I pulled into the driveway; to my left, my father was working on his car and my tubby little eight-year-old brother, Matthew, was eating a cookie. My father's marine shirt was smudged, glasses hung over his face, and his hands were covered with dirty gloves. He acknowledged me with a smile and I did the same. My brother still had not looked up from his afternoon delight. He was so invested in his cookie, the cars could have exploded and he would not have noticed.

I reached over to the passenger side and tucked the baby dog under my arm. I let myself out of my automobile and my father saw my "plus one." He pushed his glasses back into place and said, "Take it back." I quickly explained how I had obtained the dog. Still not in love with the fact I had it, he studied it and held it. "It's a boy," he said.

Matthew's face lit up and he yelled, "A puppy! What kind of dog is it, Josh?"

Both my father and I agreed it looked like a Chihuahua mixed with a wiener dog. The four of us headed inside.

For the rest of the night, complaints from my parents and sister attacked my eardrums. My sister, Marissa, who was only three years younger than I, disliked the idea of an animal in the house. Both my parents were upset because I had not informed them. No one seemed to care if the dog would die; they just wanted it gone. The arguments did not stop until Matthew was seen in the living room playing with the dog. He and the dog were happy to be rolling around on the floor together. After I saw these two bundles of joy wrestling, I looked at my parents' faces; they were not mad anymore.

As the days rolled by, I watched the dog's every move. Matthew kept asking the same question: "What is his name?" Every day I studied him and tried to be as original as possible. Small, brown, and cute, I made an imaginary list of his traits. "Bean?" I finally suggested. Matthew smiled. After I named him Bean, it felt as if he was going to be with us forever.

Everyone warmed up to Bean after a week and a half. We all began to share the responsibilities of taking care of him. I enjoyed playing tug of war with Bean, who was teething and tried to bite off my finger, but his chomp was still without strength.

On a normal Tuesday morning, the lot of us rolled out of bed and tried to wrap our heads around the early morning routines of getting to school and work. Matthew stayed in bed, not letting anyone's ruckus disturb him. I poked his back until he rolled over and looked me in the eyes. When he did, I saw that his eyes were red and puffy. My mother took the day off to get Matthew to a doctor. I took my sister and myself to school. While I was in my last class, senior English, I had Matthew on my mind, hoping he was okay. Once the bell rang, I raced to my car. My sister was already posted on the passenger side.

We opened the door of our home and saw Matthew's swelling had gone down. My mother explained: "He is allergic to dogs." My heart sank, because I knew Bean had to live with another family, and soon.

I put an ad for a home for Bean up on my Twitter page. I had a response from my friend, Alexis, within the hour. The next day I moped around and packed Bean's belongings. I knew I was doing the right thing, but I felt like falling down and crying. The drive seemed long, but once I got to Alexis's house, I wanted the drive to start over so I could spend more time with Bean. There she was, Alexis, in a yellow summer dress I had seen her wear before. She was sitting outside her small house on a porch swing, waiting for her new pet. She welcomed Bean with open arms and he buried his face in her long black hair. I saw the love she was going to give Bean and it warmed my heart.

Without me, Bean might have died that Saturday afternoon. I am glad to have spared his life. The home he has now is wondrous. Alexis has given him more affection than I could ever have. I'm glad I brought the two together.

> *Animals are property, according to some people. This is not right.*

Jaquelyn Belyeu
Instructor: Holly Batty

Dog on a Freeway

Driving to school at 7:30 a.m. is hard enough, but I was driving to school having had only three hours of sleep. As I was slogging down the 118 freeway, half asleep, and about to exit on Sepulveda, I saw in the corner of my eye a dog on the freeway divider. Without even giving it a second thought, I pulled over dangerously. Why in the world was there a dog on the freeway? How did he get here? I ran toward the dog, calling so he could hear my voice over the sounds of the cars as he began to walk into the car lanes. Thankfully I got his attention, and he very slowly started moving towards me. You could tell he was old because of the way he walked; it was with a mature stature, if that makes sense. He also looked sad, but what struck me was that he did not look scared or worried. As I struggled to get the short, yet very fluffy, old German shepherd into the car, a police car pulled up. The officer was there because of calls about this poor dog on the freeway. I asked what would happen to the dog if he were to take him. He shrugged and said he would have no choice but to take him to the pound. The pound? At the time I did not know much about pounds and how they operate, but the name alone sounded awful. So many emotions stirred up in me, so I insisted that I would take him. School was no longer part of my schedule for that day. That decision would forever alter my views and feelings toward animals. I live in a place where stray dogs are something one sees often. It was not until that day that I realized my heart was so heavy toward them, and I acted on my feelings without thinking of the danger or consequences.

Looking at this stray made my heart break. His personality grew on me quickly as I tried to get him to eat and drink some water, but nothing was successful. He easily became my focus, and I found myself giving him a name. I knew that was the number one rule of what not to do in this situation, but I could not help it. Dex was his new name, and I think he liked it. As the day went on, I was nervous yet excited to see what my parents would say about Dex. Of course I wanted to keep him; why not give him the life he should have? But my parents were not fond of coming home to a stray dog. To this day, I still do not understand why. It was such an ugly character quality I saw in my dad that night. He viewed Dex as a dirty old mutt, and he was completely grossed out that Dex was in the house. How could you look at a face like Dex's, knowing what he had gone through and have the nerve to throw him back out on the streets? I quickly began to realize that it is not a rare reaction for people to have. I stayed up late that night, thinking about Dex's owners and what kind of people they were. Of course I do not know the full story. But Dex was an old, trained dog, so he did not seem the kind to just run away. And even if he had run away, how in the world did he find himself on the freeway? Things did not add up and I was left to think the worst. People like my dad have a view that animals do not feel, and since they are not human, they do not have any rights. Animals are property, according to some people. This is not right. Animals feel pain and create bonds just as strongly as humans do. I believe that all animals that we think of as pets should be treated with more respect, especially if they are alone and vulnerable on the streets.

I knew Dex could not stay, so I had no other choice but to look into no-kill animal shelters. The next morning, I did not want to get out of bed because I knew what had to happen: I had to take Dex to a no-kill shelter in Chatsworth. As soon as I walked into the place, I felt like leaving and taking every animal with me. While the place seemed nice and fun-looking, as I walked to the back to where they keep the dogs, my heart broke as I walked past every cell. Some dogs barked angrily, other jumped with joy. But the saddest sight were the dogs that ran scared to the corner of the cage, at the sight of a human. What experience was so traumatizing that the dogs had to go running scared? As I walked out, I saw a worker put Dex into a cell. I lost control of my emotions. I am not one to cry very easily, but at that time, I could not stop. He was not barking, or crying, but the look on his face I would never forget and I still get choked up thinking about it. His beautifully aged face looked sad and defeated.

As painful as it was, I am grateful that I was put in this situation. That part of me was always there but I needed something like Dex to spark it. I made a promise to myself, as I walked away from the shelter, that once I am on my own, I will rescue as many stray animals as I can. I will do whatever I can to make sure that animals are treated with the respect and love they deserve.

To have a pet is to love something other than yourself.

Amanda Marquez

Instructor: Holly Batty

A Shaggy Dog

Our family dog, Shaggy, is now sixteen years old. He came into our lives when I was about two years old, as a late Christmas gift from my aunt and uncle. Shaggy was our family's first pet and it was hard adjusting to having another life to take care of. Shaggy was just a few months old when we got him; he had tan, curly soft fur. He is half-poodle, half-Maltese. The poodle side of him made him a bit grumpy. He had these fluffy big ears which, to this day, he hasn't grown out of. Since he was a puppy, we have never left him outside at night, so he decided it was okay to poop and pee in the house. However, he adjusted very quickly; he went from peeing near the bathroom to finally going outside. Shaggy developed a love-hate relationship with me, and to this day I don't know why. He occasionally bit me when I tried to show him love. He was hyper and a hassle and he still is, but since day one we have treated Shaggy like family, and never as just a pet.

Shaggy is getting older by the minute, and he is going blind and deaf. He can't hear the loudest noise and bumps into walls and loses balance at times. He still loves to play and run around as if he were a puppy. Every time my mom comes home, he still gets all excited, as if he hasn't seen her in years. It's funny to watch him run around, bark, and chase my mom.

As old as Shaggy is, we never expected him to be attacked in our very own backyard. The first time Shaggy was attacked was early one February morning. He came running inside as if he had seen a ghost. Since he was so frightened, we tried to calm him down and discovered he had minor cuts. We decided to take him to the vet who told us that Shaggy had been attacked, but the vet couldn't figure out what it could have been. As the months went by, we were more cautious with Shaggy going outside at certain times. We could have lost Shaggy for good. Sometime after this incident, he had to get most of his teeth pulled out because he had developed gingivitis. It was a tough time, since we had to give him medicine almost every day, but it all helped get Shaggy back to health.

When we thought everything was back to normal, we let Shaggy outside and he was attacked again. This time, it was right after the sun had gone down. I had returned from soccer practice when I saw Shaggy walking with a limp and losing his balance. He became very weak and we noticed drops of blood on the floor, trailing from the back door. I tried to lead him to his bed to lie down, but he didn't want to. My mom and I picked him up to see what was wrong and noticed his neck was dripping blood. She rushed him to the vet to see what they could do. I was terrified; I feared losing my first dog, who was family and not just a pet to me. They told my mom that he had a bruised rib and a deep cut under his throat. They also said, "This couldn't have been a raccoon…it was most likely a coyote." When they said "coyote," we couldn't believe it; a coyote roaming around North Hollywood? It seemed impossible.

Shaggy had to stay overnight at the veterinarian so they could keep an eye on him. I had been away from Shaggy before, but this time it was different; he might not wake up. They gave us the option of performing surgery or putting him to sleep. This decision was very hard for our family. We decided to have him go through surgery, knowing about all the expenses and the possibility of him not surviving. In the end, he survived. The vets were amazed at his recovery; they said, "He should have died."

Before we knew he was going to survive, my mom had told him that it was okay to let go if it was too much for his old little heart. I knew it would not feel the same if he was gone. While he stayed at the vet, the house felt empty, and I couldn't picture us losing a big part of our family. But Shaggy was a tough old dog. We were all amazed at how much better he was within the first week.

Animals come and go, but we never know when. Shaggy almost left us. We thought we would be ready for him to go because of his old age, but we were not. To have a pet is to love something other than yourself. I have had many pets besides Shaggy, but never another dog. Having a dog creates a different relationship from having a rabbit or fish. Today, when I hug Shaggy or acknowledge him, I feel love and happiness from him which makes me appreciate him more. I try to make the most of the time I spend with Shaggy and never forget how much he means to our family.

ASSIGNMENTS

What Does the Writer Say?

1. In her essay, "A Shaggy Dog," Amanda Marquez teaches a lesson about appreciation. How does she employ pathos to support her description of that lesson?

2. In "Dog on a Freeway," Jaquelyn Belyeu experiences a personal change as a result of her interaction with an animal. How does she explain that change?

What Do You Say?

3. The essay, "A Shaggy Dog," uses rich imagery in order to create scenes and invoke emotions. Identify the passages which you find the most effective and/or evocative.

4. Each of the pieces in this section about animals deals with some sort of heartache. Why do you think our relationships with animals lend themselves to such heartache? Identify one passage in each piece where pathos is used most effectively. What do those passages have in common?

Writing Exercises

5. For this exercise, write a 1–2 page reflection using "Dog on a Freeway," by Jaquelyn Belyeu, as a model:

   At the center of this essay is a split-second decision made by the author which changes her life. Have you ever been in the position where a quick decision was required? What choice did you make and how do you feel about it now?

6. For this exercise, write a 1–2 analysis on the use of pathos:

   Each of the essays in this section seem to rely on pathos to make their various points. Why do these essays make frequent use of pathos as a rhetorical strategy? Do you think this results in the most effective argument? Why or why not?

2014 New Voices Award Winner Thuy Dinh Hai Tran.

SECTION 8:
REFLECTIONS ON WRITING

QUICK WRITE:

Describe the process that you use for writing academic assignments. What steps do you take? To what extent are these steps effective? How could you improve your writing process?

Notes, Responses, & Ideas

...the act of putting my thoughts into words has always been difficult for me...

Liliana Valerio
Instructor: Emily Olson

The Perfect Storm

I remember walking onto campus on the very first day of school, heading straight for my English class and feeling as if a million dark grey clouds had appeared out of nowhere, making me feel nervous and scared, insinuating that I was in for an enormous storm. Now I sit here, less than two weeks away from the end of the first semester, feeling as if I had seen those storm clouds just yesterday. Afraid that everything I had learned in high school would be thrown out the window, I accepted all criticism and advice that poured on my shoulders from my peers and professor. As I progressed through the semester's rain, I began to feel comfortable, as most of the material taught by my professor was similar to what I had learned previously, letting me see the sunshine at the end of the storm. Having walked through the downpour and puddles of English, I feel confident about my acquired writing skills and understand that if I can see the clear blue skies, then I am ready to take on the challenges of the next storm.

For years I struggled with writing, regardless of the kind of essay I was assigned, until this semester. Finding the ideas and sources I would use was not the problem; the act of putting my thoughts into words has always been difficult for me, especially when it came to writing an introduction and elaborating on my ideas. It was not until our professor went over the basic structure and organization of an essay that I felt comfortable with writing. She explained that an introduction should contain a hook which could be an interesting statement, statistic, or anecdote; the context, which presents background information and existing theories; and a thesis statement that includes what is to be argued, how it will be proved, as well as the significance of the claim. After she explained and provided examples for each section of the essay, it was easy for me to write an introduction, which has always been the most difficult task for me to do. For example, in the rough draft of my second essay, "Marriage Decay," my introduction was very vague as it did not include very much context about my topic. However, throughout the semester this improved, especially in that essay's final draft, where I provide thorough information on the issue. The professor's explanations and examples were the rays of sunshine I needed to clear the clouds away from my potential to become a better writer.

In the same way, elaboration was difficult for me before taking this course. At the start of the semester, my method of examining and analyzing evidence was at a very basic level, as I provided simple examples of my own to reinforce the evidence, such as in the fifth paragraph of the rough draft of my third essay on Disney princesses. Now, with all the knowledge I attained throughout the semester, from one-to-one sessions to class discussions, I feel that I have improved greatly in elaborating and expanding on evidence.

Looking back at the work in my portfolio, I can see that writing three essays this semester taught me so much about writing in general and about ongoing issues in modern society. Reflecting on my semester's hard work, I see how my writing has improved. I know I am strong enough to use my recently acquired knowledge and face the challenges of my next storm.

> *In this class, however, we wrote about some pretty*
> *interesting things, and I was intrigued.*

YARELI BARAHONA

Instructor: Emily Olson

HOW ENGLISH COMPOSITION HAS HELPED ME

I am currently majoring in 'undecided.' I think I might be leaning toward biology because I'm totally into the sciences, but I have yet to figure that out. The courses I'm currently taking have shocked me by how deep they go, like my anthropology and sociology classes. English, however, is a different story. I have never liked any of the English classes I have taken, primarily because the professors made us write about subjects I had no interest in. In this class, however, we wrote about some pretty interesting things, and I was intrigued. It was a great learning process for me, and I think that my writing skills have definitely improved.

I remember writing only two essays that I truly enjoyed throughout my whole existence, one of them being in this class. The first essay I liked was a book report on the memoir, *The Glass Castle*, by Jeannette Walls, in my second year of high school. I loved the book, so when we had to do our essay, I wrote down everything I felt that needed to be said. I truly enjoyed writing that essay because I knew what I was talking about. The second essay, which I wrote in this class, was "Overpopulation Effects," based on current human population growth and its relation to the Freshman Common Reading, *The Postmortal*. I liked this essay because we were able to choose which argument we wanted to tackle and support it by providing examples and explanations.

I noticed that both essays had something in common: they were passion-driven. It occurred to me this semester that I probably did not like writing essays because I never got a detailed explanation of how to write one. My professor guided the class step by step on how to write a good essay. I understood what I had to do in this class, and that instantly made writing the essays less painful. I also felt a lot more confident writing my essays once I knew the correct structure.

How English Composition Has Helped Me

In this class, I learned that there are many components to an essay and how to piece them together effectively to produce a great essay. Never in my life had I done an annotated bibliography, but while writing my papers, I realized how helpful it is to have all of your sources cited on one page. This is one of the things I greatly appreciated learning because it helped me in this class and in my other courses as well. I think of the annotated bibliography as a pre-brainstorm for my essays because I could later choose to use the sources I picked out, or not.

Something I still have trouble with is meeting the page requirements. I did not have much experience with writing long papers before I came to college, so it all feels pretty challenging to me. I have noticed that, in this class, I have been learning how to write with more details and more explanations. For my argument essay, "Plastic Bag Ban and the Great Pacific Garbage Patch," my professor told me that in order to get my point across, I had to repeat ideas in different ways.

In-text citations and the works cited page are other essay components I never had much experience with either. This class taught me the importance of crediting my work correctly, to let the reader know the information is legitimate and to avoid plagiarism. Back in high school, my English teacher usually made us do a works cited page, but I do not remember her saying anything about in-text citations. This semester, I also attended workshops and visited the Learning Resource Center regularly to get advice on my writing assignments.

This course has helped me with the basic structure of an essay. I feel like I have definitely improved since the beginning of the semester. I have learned to expand my papers and to properly cite my work. I have also learned how to write with more descriptive details and how to rephrase my arguments in different ways to not seem repetitive but get my point across. This course was a great learning experience that gave me newfound skills.

ASSIGNMENTS

What Does the Writer Say?

1. In her essay, "The Perfect Storm," Liliana Valerio recounts the specific things she learned in her freshman composition class that have made her a better writer. What specific skills and experiences does she talk about?

2. Write an outline of Yareli Barahona's reflection, "How English Composition Has Helped Me."

What Do You Say?

3. In her reflection, "The Perfect Storm," Liliana Valerio uses imagery of clouds, skies, and storms as metaphors. Why does she choose these particular images? What metaphor would you use to describe your writing process, and why?

4. In the reflection, "How English Class Has Helped Me," Yareli Barahona seeks to tell a relatable story of learning to enjoy writing after learning to understand it. To what extent does developing an understanding change your attitude about writing?

Writing Exercises

5. In this exercise write a 1–2 page comparison of the two portfolio reflections in this section:

   In both texts, the authors make note of specific experiences they have had in English classes and what skills they have acquired. How are their experiences similar to each other? How are their experiences similar to your own? How are they different?

6. Consider your own experiences as a writer and as a student and describe what you have learned about yourself during your first semester at college. Just as Yareli Barahona explains that passion has been important to her success so far, what character trait or quality—positive or negative—has played the strongest role in your first semester?

NOTES, RESPONSES, & IDEAS

Introducing Our New Voices

Ali Alawadhi: (Online) I was born and raised in Kuwait, and I'm 19 years old. I decided to study abroad because I want to get more experiences and get out of my comfort zone. Here in California, I enjoy asking people how old I am because my face doesn't show that I'm 19 years old. I speak both Arabic and English and I've been interested in other languages. I'm planning to study other languages in the future when I have a good opportunity. I came to CSUN because last year, I was in the ESL program (English as a Second Language) at CSU, Fullerton, and one of my classmates persuaded me to apply for CSUN when he got accepted there. At that time I had already applied for many universities in the United States but I decided to add one more: CSUN. To my surprise, I got accepted at CSUN. Eventually, I decided to study at CSUN because I heard there are a lot of good teachers here. I hope to learn a lot from the university and outside the university, and get my bachelor's degree in the future.

Elizabeth Altounian: Coming into college I was nervous in general about all the aspects that college presents. For me to fit in, I felt I needed to get out of my comfort zone and put myself out there. I met so many people by doing so. I also did the same with my writing. Being a first-year college student, I did not know what to expect because I felt I was not as up to par with my writing skills as I should be coming into college. But by leaving my comfort zone, I was able to explore parts of writing that I had not done before. Writing was never my forte. Being a second language student, writing has always been a struggle for me but I learned to overcome that. I continuously pushed myself until I felt comfortable writing my thoughts in an essay. It should not be as scary a process for me as it was. I now feel comfortable getting started on an essay and it comes more naturally.

Natalie Bedrosian: I was born on January 17, 1996, in Los Angeles, California. I am a first-time freshman at CSUN, in hopes of gaining a proper education and continuously learning. I have two of the most amazing parents who have inspired me to always do my best when it comes to anything. This is what I strive for every day I wake up. I hope I can one day inspire students through my writing just like many of the students in *New Voices* have inspired me through their fantastic works.

Jaquelyn Belyeu: I am 19 years old and a freshman at CSUN. I was born here in California, but lived in Colorado for the first five years of my life. I am currently in love with sociology and psychology. I have always had a huge passion for children, and one day my dream is to get into social work. One moment that really made me want to become a social worker was when I had the opportunity to go on a missions trip to the Dominican Republic for two weeks. The purpose of this missions trip was mainly to create relationships with the Dominicans. As we arrived in the city of Jarabacoa, we began to really experience first-hand a poverty-stricken city. It was incredible to see how these beautiful people live so differently from Americans. I was stationed at the social work site of a little town called El Callejon. This small town of about 100 people had a lot of evil dwelling within. The men of El Callejon treat the women with no respect, and rarely stick to one woman. For women, it is very common to see fifteen-year-olds pregnant with their second child. Child abuse is common, as well as child prostitution. I spent my time with most of the kids (since there were so many) and learned quickly that most of them go days without eating, yet they are the most generous and selfless people I have ever met. Their smiles are still engraved in my memory to this day. I will never forget how the people of the Dominican Republic forever changed my way of thinking. That is the moment I was positive that whether I stay in the U.S, or go to countries like the Dominican Republic, this is what I am meant to do with my life. Serve, care for, bond with, and help the people who are in great need.

Muddassir Billoo: I am a Pakistani American, born in Karachi. I migrated to the United States in the second semester of 9th grade. With intense effort, I graduated as a Valedictorian of Sylmar High Leadership Academy. Currently, I am pursuing a bachelor's degree in accountancy and working at a place which plays a vital role in making Americans healthier, GNC. I am an individual who has encountered countless barriers in pursuing education in Pakistan due to financial instability. Therefore, I appreciate the opportunities that America gives to its citizens.

Alessandra Caravaggio: I am 18 years old. My favorite thing to do is laugh, because it takes away all life's troubles, even if it's only for a few minutes. I am a public health major, hoping to attend nursing school once I graduate, and I am planning on being a Spanish minor as well. I live in Simi Valley, CA, and previously attended Grace Brethren High School. I am a first-time freshman at CSUN. My first year is going great and I love it here. Being on campus is crazy for me, because I went from a private school with under 1,000 people, to a huge campus with thousands of people! Though these next few years will be very challenging, I am excited to see what they will bring to me. Once I graduate, I hope to travel to places in the world where much medical help is needed, because being a blessing to others and making them happy would bring me so much pleasure and satisfaction.

Joshua Corona: I am currently a freshman at CSUN. I like to believe I am a genuinely kind person. I enjoy being nice to everyone because it feels right. I firmly believe people should be nice to each other just for the sake of being nice; not just for a person's own selfish reasons. My passion is soccer; I live, breathe, and love the sport. My major is broadcast journalism and I hope to become a reporter or anchor for a soccer news team. It is my dream to write about soccer or talk about the sport as a career. I also hope to write a romance novel in the future because love is an incredible emotion. Love stories are my guilty pleasure.

Jing Huang. This is the first year I have studied in the United States. I participated in the 2+2 program of my university in China two years ago. This 2+2 program means after I have studied in China for two years, I will study in the United States for two years. Studying in the United States is a big challenge for me because English is not my first language, but I love English. English 113A was one of my favorite classes because I learned more about standard English writing. More importantly, my instructor taught us how to read well and how to write well. I believe that writing is an important skill for all of us.

Jeewon Lee: I am a senior exchange student majoring in psychology, and I am also interested in computer science. Last year, I applied to an exchange program from South Korea and came to the United States in order to challenge myself. Taking an English 113A class was one of my challenges. I learned more about reading and writing English than I had expected. Consequently, I now read English faster and easier; I therefore read more, such as *TIME* magazine and American newspapers. I will continue to study and learn English, as well as psychology, even though I am going to go back to my home country at the end of this semester. Of course, my main interest remains studying to become a great cognitive psychologist.

Amanda Marquez: I am a freshman at Cal State Northridge. I am 19 years old and currently studying biology. Once I finish my years at CSUN, I hope to continue my education in medical school. I am currently working at Macy's and on days off, I like to volunteer. I used to volunteer at Valley Presbyterian and hope to go back for the winter. I am shy at first, but even with the shyness, I am outgoing and fun. I have also played soccer for almost 14 years and try to play any chance I get. While at CSUN, so far I have made many friends and the memories to go along. I hope to achieve my goals at CSUN while still enjoying my time in college.

Emanuel Moreno-Valdez: I was born and raised in a rural area in the central part of Mexico. When I was 15 years old, I immigrated to the U.S. without knowing any English. My family and I settled in a small town near Fresno, CA, called Cutler-Orosi and I was enrolled in Orosi High School. My family always has wanted me to study in a university, and the United States offers plenty of opportunity for minorities, like me, to continue with an academic career. My math and science teachers from high school encouraged me to pursue an engineering degree because those were my two strongest subjects. However, surprisingly, I also became a good writer and reader. During my senior year, I decided to pursue a civil engineering degree, and CSUN has a really good engineering program so I decided to come here.

Moises Navarrete: I'm from Compton, CA, and I'm nineteen years old. I am currently undecided of what my major is going to be, but I'm leaning towards becoming an English major. Music was my first option, but seeing how much English has interested me in the past semester, I feel more comfortable going into that area. My purpose of being in college is more than just to get a degree and get out of here; my parents have had the biggest impact on me being here, so I'm striving to provide for their future as they have for mine.

Kayla Nehorayan: I am a freshman at CSUN majoring in Nutrition and Dietetics. I am 19 years old and graduated from Sierra Canyon High School in Chatsworth, CA, in 2013. After graduating, instead of going to University of Arizona as I planned, I took a gap year and worked at Williams-Sonoma. I received so much experience that I decided I wanted to go to school and get my degree. My first semester at CSUN has been incredible so far. Not only have I made so many friends in all my classes, but I also joined a sorority and have received great grades in my classes. I cannot wait for next semester to begin, to eventually graduate, and start doing what I love.

Trang Nguyen: I am 19 years old and I am currently a freshman. I was born and raised in Vietnam, but immigrated to the United States three years ago. Coming to the United States, I experienced many new things. There is a huge difference between cultures, weather, law, and especially language. English is a barrier which limits my communication with others. I put in more effort than others because I know I am not a native speaker. Writing essays is challenging for me. I have to keep my eyes open to grammar and wording in an essay. Although I face a lot of struggles, I never give up on writing and learning English. I tell myself to hold my head up high and look for success. In order to obtain that wish, I push myself to work harder. I never mind judgments from others. I take that as advice to complete and develop myself. I make a lot of handmade items and I love to use my free time to do so. Going to CSUN, I have been given a special opportunity to pursue my dream job. It's a long journey, but I will not stop walking, and climbing until I reach the highest mountain.

Marc Ninapaytan: I am currently 18 years old and was born in the city of Hawthorne, CA. I am of Peruvian descent and am a proud gay man. Throughout my life I've faced plenty of obstacles, as any regular person does. What truly makes me stand out is my ability to express all of these memories and horrendous, yet uplifting obstacles, through my writing. Not many can do that. Trust me when I say it isn't easy. Honestly, it took me a while to make myself vulnerable when I write, which is what I think makes my writing easy to read, relatable, and as some may say, inspirational. However, there are many LGBTQA people who have gone through similar struggles as I have. My true objective is for other young students to read and write more LGBTQA literature. Through overcoming obstacles, the LGBTQA community will continue to flourish and will help to create a future that's equal for everyone.

Arely Flores Osorio: (Online) I was born and raised in Los Angeles, CA. I am currently an undergraduate attending CSU Northridge, majoring in psychology and planning to do a minor in English. I enjoy writing poems and short stories. In 10th grade, I participated in a talent show sponsored by Samahang Pilipino Advancing Community Empowerment (SPACE) at UCLA. I was able to recite one of my poems. After I recited my poem, I started to reflect that I have a passion toward writing. I continue to write poems and short stories during my free time.

Angela Pham: I'm a freshman majoring in health administration and intending to get into the BSN program here at CSUN. I lean more toward the science field, but I do very much enjoy English as well. In my free time, I love to be with friends/family, journalize my life, do taekwondo, art, play golf, and experience new things. I am a very open-minded person and easily approachable. Being here at CSUN makes me overwhelmed and excited, because all the steps that lead up to my career are here on campus.

Pegah Poordehghan: I was born on July 14, 1996. I am a freshman at CSUN, and so far the college experience has been great. I am a psychology major, hoping to stay at CSUN for my master's because CSUN has a great social science program. I am excited to continue my education at CSUN because I really enjoy the campus and the environment more than I thought I would, and it is very close to home. My dream job is to become a clinical psychologist one day and have my own office. Moving from Iran to the United States as a third grader was tough and every day was a challenge. Having to adapt to a completely new country in such a short time was complicated and school was always challenging and never fun. However that did not stop me from doing my best and trying my hardest. The challenges helped me to prove to myself that I am capable of handling challenging situations.

Lorena Robertson: I am a freshman majoring in accounting. I grew up in the San Fernando Valley and attended San Fernando High School. I come from a very tight-knit family of five. I am the youngest with three sisters, one brother, and two nieces. I believe that family is everything you need because they are the ones who will never leave your side. I value spending time with my family since we don't often see my sister who lives in San Francisco, or my brother because he is serving our country. In my essay you will see how family plays a big role in who I am today. Hope you enjoy!

Catalina Roldan: "Where are you from? I love your accent!" Every time some-one asks me where I come from, I proudly tell them, "I am from Colombia, South America." Apparently, my physical appearance confuses Americans because I have light skin and blue eyes. The fact that people confuse my nationality amuses me. Little do they know how challenging it was for me to learn English at all. My name is Catalina; I was born and raised in Colombia but moved to the United States in 2009. I sincerely wanted to learn English when I came to Mulholland Middle School, so I tried my best for two hours, every day, for six months, in an English Learner's class. I was surrounded by an Hispanic community which I hoped would welcome me. However, students would not accept that a light-skinned, blue-eyed Colombian was not bilingual. At that point, I barely spoke English at all. Now that I look back, middle school was where I learned about the real world. And at that time it seemed to be hell in every aspect. In the summer of 2010, I was accepted by lottery enroll-ment to HTLA High School, and my world flipped 360 degrees…in a positive way. The best part was the teachers and administrators, who were caring and understanding. HTLA's teachers not only helped with my English skills, but they believed in me and gave me confidence to keep pushing forward through assignments that were difficult. Currently, I am attending CSUN and with the same purpose and willingness to keep learning and moving forward with my studies, the journey continues.

Liliana Valerio: I am a first-time freshman at CSUN. Being born and raised in Northridge, California, it only seemed logical to come to CSUN. Ever since I was in elementary school, I would come to CSUN on fieldtrips to the Performing Arts Center to watch plays. In my free time, I like to spend time with my family or listen to music. Although I am an undecided major, I know that CSUN will be a major part of helping me achieve any aspirations I develop throughout my educational career, such as perhaps becoming a zoologist. While I know achieving any career can be tough, I plan to face any and every challenge presented to me with the grit that will help me achieve a successful career and make my parents proud.

Dianna Zaragoza: I am a first-time freshman at CSUN. I am the fourth child in my immediate family, and the first to go to a university. I am majoring in psychology but am considering if I should change it. I want to become a forensic psychologist and to do that, I would need to major in political science and minor in psychology. I want to work with criminal cases in court rooms. I am of Hispanic background and also the only child left in the household. I know that in order to get to where I want to be, I would have to work hard, stay ambitious, and ultimately focus on my studies. I have overcome obstacles that have ultimately made me a strong person and for any students in high school who feel convinced they can't, I am here to tell you that I was in your shoes, and l know you can do it. Everyone is capable of achieving their complete greatness.